AN EXPE
OF *Spirit*

SPIRITUALITY *and*
STORYTELLING

John Shea

Liguori
LIGUORI, MISSOURI

Imprimi Potest:
Thomas D. Picton, C.Ss.R.
Provincial, Denver Province
The Redemptorists

Published by Liguori Publications
Liguori, Missouri
www.liguori.org

Library of Congress Cataloging-in-Publication Data

Shea, John, 1941–.
    An experience of Spirit : spirituality and storytelling / John Shea.—Rev. ed.
        p. cm.
    Rev. ed. of: An experience named Spirit.
    Includes bibliographical references (p. 231).
    ISBN 0-7648-1287-4
    1. Love—Religious aspects—Christianity. 2. Jesus Christ—Person and offices. 3. Spiritual life—Christianity. 4. Storytelling—Religious aspects—Christianity. I. Shea, John, 1941– Experience named Spirit. II. Title.

BV4639.S49 2005
248.4'82—dc22   2005040788

The editor/publisher gratefully acknowledge permission to reprint/reproduce copyrighted works granted by the publishers/sources listed on page 239.

Liguori Publications, a nonprofit corporation, is an apostolate of the Redemptorists. To learn more about the Redemptorists, visit *Redemptorists.com*.

Printed in the United States of America
09 08 07 06 05   5 4 3 2 1
Revised edition 2005

Contents

Preface

RAY HART has remarked that prefaces are "What-It's-All-About in a few words in advance of the many." That is undoubtedly true. A preface should not "give the book away," but it can "let the reader in" on the style and themes of the pages to follow. In a book about spirituality and storytelling, a story from the rabbis is always a good place to begin.

⁜⁜⁜

Two Brothers

Two brothers shared a farm. One brother was married and had seven children. The other brother was single. They worked hard and the land was good. Each year the harvest was abundant; and each year they split the wealth of the land evenly. They gathered the perfectly divided grain into their separate barns and thanked God for his goodness.

One night the single brother thought to himself: "It is not right that we should divide the grain evenly. My brother has many mouths to feed and he needs more. I have only myself to look after. I can certainly get by with less." So each night the single brother would take grain from his barn and secretly transfer it to the barn of his married brother.

That same night the married brother thought to himself: "It is not right that we should divide the grain evenly. I have many children who will look after me in my old age. My brother has only himself. Surely he will need to save more for the future." So each night the married brother would take grain from his barn and secretly transfer it to the barn of his single brother.

Each night the brothers gave away their grain. Yet each morning they found their supply mysteriously replenished. They never told each other about this miracle.

Then one night they met each other half way between the barns. They realized at once what had been happening. They embraced each other with laughter and tears.

On that spot they built the Temple.

⠪⠕

This is a book about divine and human love. It explores how the two are interwoven, how the human mediates the divine and how the divine suffuses the human. It explores the resistance of the human and the persistence of the divine. Both are not what they seem. They are more.

This book about stories also explores how contemporary life stories interact with inherited stories, and how the hearing of inherited stories uncovers the depth of present experience and funds the future. Most of all, it is about the story of Jesus and the experience of life that it communicates.

Jesus was the catalyst of a salvific experience, the bearer of divine salvation. Jesus now lives in the far reaches of God; but the experience which he inaugurated did not "ascend heavenward" with him. It continued among his followers who called themselves the Body of Christ, the ongoing possibility of salvation. The transmission of Christian faith is incurably people-centered, dependent upon the press of flesh from generation to generation. But no matter how many years distance us from Jesus, we will not forget him. His life, death, and resurrection is the authentic revelation of the living relationship to God.

The upshot of all this, as chapter one suggests, is that we are a People of Spirit and Memory.

The soul of the People of Spirit and Memory is their living relationship with God, which is activated by the experience of Spirit. This foundational experience is explosive. It inspires the human mind and heart to myriad creations. The People of Spirit and Memory have produced myths and rituals, elaborated beliefs and theologies, espoused values and behaviors. As generation succeeds generation, these diverse creations stockpile. They are in constant need of reform in order to be faithful to the living God they reflect.

The principle is that the Church is always reforming, but never fully reformed. The creations of the People of Spirit and Memory have many different and very important functions, but only one ultimate purpose. They are expressions of the salvific experience of Spirit and are meant to facilitate that experience for all who come in contact with them. At least that is what chapter two seems to think.

A preeminent creation of the people of Spirit and Memory is narrative. Story is the one of the primal expressions of the experience of Spirit; and Christian faith regularly retells its sacred stories. The great hope of every retelling is that the tale will powerfully intersect the life of the hearers; and they will experience, however dimly, the reality of Spirit.

The second half of chapter three explores the dynamic of hearing the sacred stories of the tradition. But those stories are old and these are secular times (so the propaganda runs). People are interested in their own personal stories. We must begin with contemporary stories and bring forward the story of Jesus, the premier sacred story of Christianity, to interpret the depth of what is happening. So the first half of chapter three starts with personal narrative and merges it with the sacred stories of the tradition. The great hope remains the same—that in the merger of the two stories the experience of Spirit will emerge.

Chapter four probes the abiding concerns of the experience of Spirit. If this experience, and the living relationship to
God it activates, is the connection between Christ and Church,
the source and goal of the creations of the Christian tradition,
and the ambition of Christian storytelling, what does this experience entail?

The first moment of the experience of Spirit is an inrush of
divine love mediated by human love. This love seeks and finds
the heart of each person. More often than not, our hearts are
living in either rejection or envy. For the rejected, this love sets
a table; for the envious, this love holds up a mirror. For both, it
offers the opportunity for another way of being human.

The mystery of iniquity is that our hearts kill the love that
seeks to save us. But this divine love does not give up. The
crucifixion of love becomes the everlasting offer of new life. Of
course, Jesus, the Son of God, is the one who revealed all this
to us.

The first moment of the experience of Spirit is the swift
inrush of divine love. The second moment is the stumble of
human response. What will we do with the Love that loves us
more than we love ourselves? Chapter five struggles with a few
suggestions. The surrender to divine love liberates human love.

This human love moves in two directions at once—toward
God and toward neighbor. Both these directions are intimately
bound together. Love for God means praying and plotting and
holding on; unless, of course, letting go is what is called for.
Loving God is the ultimate adventure. Loving our neighbor in
God is the proximate passion. To love the neighbor is to see
their well-deserved injuries as our own undeserved wounds. It
also entails a reversal of personal power. It is no longer inge-
niously employed for personal gain, but lavishly spent for human reconciliation. The experience of Spirit results in joyous
struggle. Of course, Jesus, brother to us all, is the revelation of
this struggle.

Even in minor moments of honesty, anyone writing a book admits he or she is talking to himself or herself. The primary audience is the writer's soul. But hopefully they are soul mates. They are envisioned as people who are trying to think and live faith to the full; who know that genuine religious living is the key to what Kazantzakis called the "luminous interval between birth and death"; who have a heritage they honor, but wish they understood more deeply; who want to say something to the next generation but want to make sure it comes from their heart; who believe in more than they have experienced but want to experience most of what they believe; who want to allow religious truth to illumine interpersonal and social life but reject simplicism and fanaticism; and who know that complexity and struggle are the name of the game but who party like five-year-olds whenever hope arrives. If these feelings shape your soul, welcome.

AN EXPERIENCE
OF *Spirit*

Chapter One

A People of Spirit and Memory

The matter of the fact is that we can contact Jesus only through the Church. The decision of faith can take place within her alone, because she alone supplies us with the situation basic to faith, contemporaneity.[1]

ROMANO GUARDINI

Nine Catholic Christians were gathered in a home on the northwest side of Chicago. They were discussing the condition of their parish and the changes they hoped would come about. One of the more zealous members of the group opened a Bible which throughout the conversation sat on her lap like an obedient cat. She began, "Jesus says here that…" But she got no further. The man sitting next to her reached over and with a flick of his hand flipped the Bible shut.

"Why are you reading in the presence of Christ?" he asked angrily.

The man who so unceremoniously closed the Holy Book

1

in favor of the Holy Company spoke one of Christianity's most daring claims: "Christ is present." Jesus Christ is not only the past founder of our relationship to God but also its present mediator. He not only overcame the law of time by not being forgotten, he overcame the law of death by not being lost. He lives among us! And our rhetoric for his presence ranges from the lyrical Gerard Manly Hopkins' verse "Christ plays in ten thousand places" to the sudden, shocking revelation of Zooey Glass in J. D. Salinger's *Catcher in the Rye*, "And don't you know—listen to me now—don't you know who that fat lady really is?...Ah, buddy. Ah, buddy. It's Christ himself. Christ himself, buddy."

What are we to make of this? How are we to understand the contemporary presence of Jesus Christ? How do we have access to Jesus Christ today? And how is that access related to the long-ago historical personage of Jesus of Nazareth and the witness to him that we have in the New Testament?

People, Always People

At Christmastime throughout the Christian world a truly remarkable event takes place. Parents and children stand before crib scenes and take note of what is represented. Three-year-old fingers point to the center of the scene and ask, "Who's that?" "Baby Jesus" is the time-honored reply. "And who's that?" No three-year-old settles for one question or one answer. "His mother Mary. And that's his foster father, Joseph. And those are the shepherds and those are the Wise Men."

So it goes. The newest generation is beginning to hear about Jesus.

Charles Peguy highlighted this same experience of passing on the meaning and message of Christ.

Just as at the church door,
    on Sundays and feast days,
When we go to Mass,
Or at funerals,
We pass holy water to each other from hand to hand,
One to another, one after the other,
To make the sign of the cross, upon ourselves,
The living, or on the coffins of the dead,
So that step by step the same sign of the cross is,
    as it were,
    carried by the same water....
In the same way, from hand to hand,
    from fingers to fingers,
From finger-tip to finger-tip,
    the everlasting generations
Who go to Mass age after age,
One generation succeeding another,
Pass on the word of God, in the same hope,
In the same breasts, in the same hearts,
    until the world itself is buried....[2]

So it goes. From the fingers of one to the fingers of another, the word of God makes its way through history.

In Robert Browning's poem "A Death in the Desert," the apostle John is dying. He reflects on his life until the end comes, and he "lies as he lay once, breast to breast with God." One of his musings concerns his role as the last living witness to Jesus Christ.

If I live yet, it is for good, more love
Through me to men: be nought but ashes here
That keep awhile my semblance, who was John.
Still, when they scatter, there is left on earth
No one alive who knew (consider this!)

—Saw with his eyes and handled with his hands
That which was from the first, the Word of Life.
How will it be when none more saith "I saw?"[3]

The entire Christian tradition is an answer to that final question—"How will it be when none more saith 'I saw'?" This is
how it will be—people will tell others what those who saw told
them. They will remember and tell the next generation.

This fact dictates the beginning of any contemporary retelling of the story of Jesus. It must start with: "I never saw
him. I never heard him. I never touched him. But there were
those who did. And they told others, who told others, who
told others still, who eventually told me. And now, in my turn,
I tell you. And you, then, can tell others. And so, you see,
there will never be an end to it."

Catholic Christianity stresses that access to the original
long-ago event of Jesus Christ is mediated through people. It
cultivates a romantic vision of hands clasping hands, linking
backward through time until they touch the hand of Jesus
Christ, who holds the hand of God. The conversational flow
of this long, historical line is largely one-sided. The older generation confides to the younger generation the sufferings and
glories of Jesus Christ, the Son of God and Savior of the World.

What is important is not the bare fact that the conversation takes place, but what happens between the people who
tell and listen to the story of Jesus Christ. Therefore, present-
day contact with Jesus Christ occurs through a chain of people
stretching over nineteen hundred years; and, of course, people
being people, the pervading fear is that with each added link
the chain grows weaker.

Each generation of Christians, since the first, has preserved
the memory of Jesus and, as best they could, lived within, acted
out of, and passed on his Spirit. Tradition is a premeditated
act of fragile people not wanting to lose what they love.

This insistence that people are the ultimate carriers and communicators of the Christ event is hinted at by Paul in the Second Letter to the Corinthians. When some require of him a letter of recommendation, he points to the community itself as a "letter of Christ...written not with ink but with the Spirit of the living God, not on tablets of stone but on the tablets of human hearts" (3:3).

Human hearts that have been written on by the Spirit of the living God become a communication from Christ to other people. This is why Walter Kasper insists that "faith in Jesus Christ can arise only from encounter with believing Christians."[4]

It may seem banal to stress that it is people, always people, who bring us into contact with Jesus Christ. But it is a fact that is easily forgotten. We tend toward "false objectivisms" which give the impression that Christ arrives independent of his flawed followers. We say we reach Christ through the Scriptures. But what is the New Testament but the witnessing words of people who had to speak of what they found through Jesus of Nazareth?

We say Christ is present in the sacraments. But what are the sacraments but the creations and re-creations of people bent on continuing the salvific experience Jesus inaugurated?

We say Christ is present in the Church. But what is the Church but the collectivity of us all, the master and the slave, the Jew and the Gentile, this man and that woman who are mysteriously united, beyond the differences that divide them? The messy truth is that Christ comes to us finger-printed by every generation that ever embraced him.

To stress the people-grounding of Scripture, sacraments, and Church is not meant to slight the presence of God in Christ in these realities. This is an attempt to recognize and underline the fact that Scripture, sacraments, and Church are ventures of divine-human cooperation. They are the divinely inspired creations of people who have become the privileged locale of contact with God.

Christ is present in Word, sacrament, and Church. But to say that Christ is present we do not have to say that we are not present. The history of Scripture, sacraments, and Church show that they have been created, participated in, reinterpreted, and reformed by people. A nonnegotiable of the human condition is the co-presence of the divine and the human. If we would hear the thunderous voice of God, we must attend to human mumblings.

That people pass on the faith is intimately related to the "essence" of what is to be passed on. The essence of Christian faith is not a message, so it is not enough to hear and understand what Jesus said and did. Neither is the essence a series of ethical mandates, so it is not enough to strive for the perfection the Gospels outline.

The essence of Christian faith is a living relationship with God, a relationship which was inaugurated by Jesus of Nazareth and which is presently available through his Spirit as it suffuses and transforms the lives of his followers. From this relationship there emerged and continues to emerge, as surface waters of a lake are refreshed by hidden springs, a message and an ethic. But without the experience of the lived relationship to God, the message becomes gibberish and the ethic becomes folly.

If the content of Christian faith is ultimately the relationship to God, which originated in the divine-human event of Jesus Christ, then what better way to pass it on than in the divine-human events that are our encounters with one another? Perhaps our language about faith is too "treasure"-oriented. We call it an inheritance and tend to envision it as a sack of gold handed down from generation to generation. Much truth about Christian faith can be wrung from this metaphor, but it can also give the false impression that faith is a "thing" to be protected and prized. This "crown jewels" approach tends to engender an attitude of vigilant defense. We become defenders of the faith and beat off people who approach it with new ideas. We caricature them as motivated by plunder and desecration. Most often, they have merely come to talk.

Is not, however, the deeper Christian instinct toward faith and its transmission an attitude of invitation and hosting? Those who enjoy a relationship with the God of Jesus invite others into a relationship with themselves. In and through these relationships, which are resourced and critiqued by the Spirit, the possibility of entering into a relationship with the God of Jesus emerges. The present company of believers hosts new people, both searching adults and growing children, into their life together, and through this life into the abundant life which flows from God. In this way faith is passed on.

This "people focus" is the perspective behind John Coventry's answer to the question, "What in fact is handed on by the Church?"

> The radical answer to this question [...] may seem at first sight very inward-looking. The radical answer can only be, THE CHURCH. The living Church hands on, perpetuates in history, the living Church. The Church, one might say, is history; it is living and believing men and women, perpetuating their faith in succeeding generations, and expressing it in manifold ways.[5]

"The living Church hands on the living Church" might be taken as classic Catholic arrogance suggesting that the Church has no larger reality it must be faithful to. It is its own reward. But purged of this distortion, Coventry's statement does touch upon the interpersonal truth of Christian religion. Men and women of today in their extravagance and timidity, their cowardice and courage, their sacrificial love and self-giving schemes somehow continue what Jesus began. They make Christ present anew in every age.

The best way to understand this incorrigible and corruptible "peopleness" of Christian faith and its transmission is to return to the beginning. We must explore the experiential and relational reality that is at the heart of that faith. This reality is summed up in the phrase "Jesus Christ."

Jesus Christ

The words *Jesus Christ* refer to an interpersonal event initiated by Jesus of Nazareth and received by the people he encountered. In relationship to Jesus, people contacted the transformative power of divine reality. One response to this mediated encounter with God was to call Jesus "the Christ, the Anointed One." It is interesting to note that Jesus did not call himself the Christ. Although Jesus had a definite consciousness of himself and his mission, it is difficult to tell if he ever used any titles for himself. But where he was reluctant, others were eager. It was the people who were saved through Jesus who bestowed the titles. *Jesus Christ* designates the relational flow between Jesus of Nazareth and his followers. It is Christian code, a compressed way of talking about an experience which the Gospel of John suggests could not be compressed into all the books ever written.

This interpersonal focus on the core Christian reality is important to maintain. In the first place, it reflects the fullness of the scriptural accounts. The New Testament writings are deeply relational documents, creations of transformed witnesses rather than neutral observers of the Jesus scene. Although it is important at times to distinguish the historical Jesus from the Christ of faith, it is even more important to hold them together as the full expression of the saving encounter.[6] Willie

Marxsen, in examining the structure of the Gospels, states this point strongly:

> The primal datum of the church is therefore not a person, but rather a relationship starting from this person. ...To put it more exactly, we would have to say that Jesus and the one who believes belong together....This means...that the beginnings of Christology...lie at the point where the relationship between Jesus and the believer becomes visible for the first time.[7]

The Gospels, as they stand, give us neither an isolated Jesus nor an isolated believer, but the fire and ice between them.

A second perspective on the interpersonal origins of Christian faith concerns the way our interest moves "from presence to person." In the presence of some people, we feel enhanced. Life is richer when we are with them; life is poorer when we are away from them. If this is the case, we want to know more about them. We try to uncover the mystery of their impact on us. We pursue the uniqueness of their person because of the uniqueness of their presence. Our interest in them is piqued because of what they are able to generate in us when we are with them. The blunt fact of relational life is that we do not seek out the "person" of those people who, as the wag puts it, "when they enter a room, it is like someone has left." When Jesus entered the room, something happened.

In regard to Jesus, this simple process is captured in the story of the tempest at sea (Mark 4:35–41). Jesus and his disciples are in the boat. Jesus is asleep. A storm comes up. The disciples are terrified. They wake Jesus and ask him to help. He rebukes them for their lack of faith, then calms the winds and sea. In this situation the disciples ask, "Who is this that even the winds and sea obey him?" The suggestion is that if Jesus had been washed overboard, they would never have asked.

The question of inner, religious identity (the individual's ultimate relationship to God) becomes important when the relational reality between people becomes salvific.

The theological rendition of this "interest dynamic" is that
soteriology is temporally prior to christology.[8] The salvific
impact that Jesus had on people precedes the question of his
identity. Who he is becomes important because of what he is
doing.

> It was not Jesus who was important but what he DID,
> what he BROUGHT, what EVENT OCCURRED through
> him, what he SET IN MOTION. Nevertheless, what HE
> did, what HE brought, what HE effected was also im-
> portant but HE was not important apart from his DEEDS.
> In short, the conviction of the first witnesses was: Jesus
> actualizes God.[9]

This emphasis does not lessen the importance of Christology
nor relegate it to the realm of afterthought. It merely stresses a
developmental rather than a logical pattern. The logical approach of much classical thinking about Jesus established his
personal identity in relationship to the Father and then pro-
ceeded to a consideration of his saving work. The contemporary developmental approach begins with his saving power and
moves to the God-grounded source of that power. In both approaches soteriology and Christology must be tightly held together.

When we consider the relational reality that Jesus generated, it is especially necessary to move to the mystery of his
person. This movement is more than just a "next step," a logical unfolding of a fascinating presence. It comes as an imperative from the experience itself. The level on which Jesus
interacted with people forced them to focus on his deepest
identity and on their own.

Given the central witness that the encounter with Jesus was salvific, the question is often asked: "What was it about Jesus that mediated the divine? Did he speak the words of God?" Yes, but more. "Did he do the deeds of God?" Yes, but more.

It was the very person of Jesus, his core self, a self constituted by his intimate relationship to God whom he called "Abba," that made the divine accessible. In the images of the New Testament, Jesus is not only the Word of God and the Servant of God, he is also the Son of God. The metaphor of Son points to the centered self, the inner, foundational constitution of the person. Meeting Jesus meant more than exchanging words or sharing actions. The encounter moved through words and actions to their secret source, two people personally present to each other. In this situation divine reality, who Edward Schillebeeckx once called the transcendent third in every relationship, also appears.[10]

The most profound appreciation of the event of Jesus Christ is that it is an "I-thou" encounter. Jesus interacted with people in such a way that their core self came in contact with his own; and this contact was an invitation to participate in his salvific structure of selfhood. That is why Christians call themselves, "sons and daughters in the Son." Who they are is indebted to the One who reached them at the level of sonship and daughtership and reconstructed their identity to conform to his own.

In the history of Church reflection, Jesus will eventually be confessed as the second Person of the Trinity. This confession acknowledges the true revelatory center of the event of Jesus Christ. It occurs on the deepest level of the self, the level where personhood is constructed. The event of Jesus Christ is preeminently an occurrence of "person calling out to person."

The Real Absence and the New Presence

From this relational perspective, the crucial events of the origins of Christianity concern the presence and absence of the person of Jesus. John Bowker suggests that the core religious problem of Jesus' day was the question of theistic effect, discerning "God's effect in the world." For this problem there were many proposed solutions. Jesus' solution was "literally idiocentric."

> For what is clearly suggested by the surviving evidence is that Jesus offered his own self as the solution to the problem; or perhaps more accurately one should say that Jesus seems to have located the solution to the problem first and foremost in his own person, and that it was in and through his own person that he claimed to be mediating God's effect in the world.[11]

If this is true, the loss of Jesus is of immeasurable consequence. When he is present, God is saving the people. When he is absent, God has drawn back into the sky. The near God is the far God once again. And the people are abandoned.

The ascension narrative in the Book of Acts is the clearest expression we have of the loss of Jesus. What must be remembered is that this is the second time the disciples have lost him. They knew him in the "days of his flesh" and lost him to death. Then they knew him, at least some of them, in the "days of his glory"—the resurrection appearances—and lost him to the transcendent realm of God.

In different language, they knew Jesus as both a physical and spiritual body and were not able to hold on to him in either form. In the total picture of Luke-Acts, the ascension narratives function to close one era and open another. In the

Gospel of Luke, the ascension ends the story of Jesus; in the Book of Acts, it begins the story of the Church. But this transition is not without apprehension.

The two men in white who interpret the meaning of the ascension say, "Men of Galilee, why do you stand looking up toward heaven? This Jesus, who has been taken up from you into heaven, will come in the same way as you saw him go into heaven" (Acts 1:10).

Much is implied in these words. The disciples are not to worry about the destiny of Jesus. He is with God and, at the appointed time, he will come from God. They should be about the mission that has been entrusted to them.

This is certainly sound advice. But it may be that it is precisely the mission that they are worrying about as they watch Jesus disappear into the clouds. If the mission is more than just telling people about Jesus, if it entails initiating people into the relationship with God which Jesus made possible, then how is this going to be done if Jesus is not here to do it? To extend the image of ascension, one can fantasize that it was not curiosity that made them stare, but panic. If they could have, they would have reached up and pulled Jesus back to earth by his heels. What they were watching move ever farther away from them was the One who made it possible for them to love one another. What will happen now that he is gone?

"As he departs, so will he come" proves to be scant consolation. The Parousia is delayed; and many scholars think its failure to arrive is the overriding dilemma of early Christianity. But viewed from a Lukan perspective, it is the tail end of the situation created by the ascension. The hope for a Second Coming springs, in part, from the heartbreak of a second leaving. The proclamation of Jesus' exaltation to the right hand of the Father pointed to the bittersweet experience of his not being in the company of his friends.

With the loss of the person of Jesus, both in his earthly

and risen state, came the fear that the salvific experience he mediated would also go away. As Boniface Willems states it, "Christ died, and 'a cloud took him out of [our] sight' (cf. Acts 1:9). During the twenty centuries which have passed since then a huge mass of clouds has built up."[12] He is gone.

Of course, the fullness of Christian faith has more to say. The resurrection-ascension-exaltation experience is both a statement about Jesus' personal destiny with God and his continued companionship with his followers. But this should not be quickly rushed into. It is easy to slip into a "Christ is present" rhetoric, which does not give sufficient attention to the radically different forms of presence.

> The significance of this central tenet of the faith of the apostolic Church (Jesus is Lord) lies in her confident and optimistic conviction that Jesus Christ through His exaltation to the Father's right hand has not been removed to some mythical existence beyond the furthest galaxy, but is actually more dynamically present in the world than ever He was when He walked the hills of Galilee....This unshakable belief of the apostolic Church explains a noteworthy feature of the entire New Testament, an outlook particularly prominent in the theological attitudes of the four Evangelists. Search as you will, you will discover in their books no nostalgia for "the good old days."[13]

The optimism and confidence of statements like this bolster our trust in the first witnesses to Christ. But they leave little room for tears.

Yet there must have been, if not tears, the ache that accompanies waiting for the one they love to return. The disciples may not have longed for "the good old days" but they did long for "the good new days" when he would be with them again. When this Second Coming did not occur, his presence through the Spirit received more attention. Although there is real continuity between presence of Jesus in his physical body, in his resurrected body, and in the Spirit, there is also difference—vast difference, painful difference.

Real loss must be acknowledged. The man who made mud for the eyes of the blind and inserted his fingers into the ears of the deaf, who ate and drank, wept and shouted, argued and prayed, who told stories and kept strangely silent, died and rose—that man is gone. Gone in glory, according to believers, but gone nonetheless.

The Jesus whose feet could be anointed by perfume and whose hands could be pierced by nails is no longer among us the way he once was. His Spirit continues his presence, but it is manifestly not the same. Those first friends he left behind cried, "*Maranatha!*" Come, Lord Jesus! It may have been a plea for the victors to come back and vanquish their foes. But it may also have been the heartfelt cry that love lets out for reunion. In fact, it may be the Spirit itself, the presence of Jesus in one way, calling to the Risen Lord, the presence of Jesus in another way.

There is always a poignancy about Christian faith, a yearning for the Missing One. The way to understand the perennial presence of Christ is to recognize the absence of Jesus. The real absence must precede the new presence. This new and distinctive presence is captured most powerfully in the images of "bequeathing the Spirit" and "Body of Christ." To explore these images is to penetrate the paradox: the One who is gone is with us all days, even until the end of time.

The Spirit of Christ

Chapters thirteen to seventeen of the Gospel of John is a reading by the soon-to-be-deceased Jesus of his last will and testament.[14] To overhear this final conversation between Jesus and his friends, even with its heavy theological accents, is to sense its emotional power.

> My little children
> I shall not be with you much longer.
> You will look for me
> And where I am going
> You cannot come.

His friends will search for Jesus (once again this hints at the depth and poignancy of their loss); but they will not find him. He must journey to a far place and they cannot accompany him. Yet in the vision of the Johannine Christ even this loss turns to gain.

> I will not leave you orphans...
> You are sad at heart.
> Still I must tell you the truth:
> It is for your own good that I am going
> Because unless I go
> The advocate will not come to you;
> but if I do go,
> I will send him to you.

Jesus must leave but the Spirit, sent from both Jesus and the Father, will arrive. So the heartbreak of departure gives way, not only to the hope of reunion—"In a short time you will no longer see me / And then a short time later you will see me again"—but also to a new form of presence.

> The Spirit will glorify me
> Since all he tells you
> Will be taken from what is mine.
> Everything the Father has is mine;
> That is why I said:
> All he tells you
> Will be taken from what is mine.

The initial resolution to the absence of Jesus is the giving of the Spirit. Since this Spirit is the Spirit of Jesus, it becomes a guarantor of his presence in a new way; and through his presence the salvific experience he initiated. As Ray Brown succinctly puts it, "John presents the Paraclete as the Holy Spirit in a special role, namely, as the personal presence of Jesus in the Christian while Jesus is with the Father."[15]

James Dunn spells out this function of the Spirit in the Gospel of John in illuminating detail.

> The lengthening time gap between John and the historical Jesus and the continuing delay of the parousia does not mean a steadily increasing distance between each generation of Christians and the Christ. On the contrary, each generation is as close to Jesus as the last—and the first—because the Paraclete is the immediate link between Jesus and his disciples in every generation. That is to say, the link and the continuity is provided not by sacraments or offices or human figures, but by the Spirit. The vitality of Christian experience does not cease because the historical Jesus has faded into the past and the coming of Jesus has faded into the future; it retains its vitality because the Spirit is at work here and now as the other Paraclete. (Jesus is the first Paraclete.)[16]

We are now in the land of bold assertions. Peter looked into the eyes of Jesus; we have never seen his face. Yet we have as intimate an access to him as Peter. The disciples sat at the feet of Jesus and listened to his words; we have never heard his voice. Yet he is present to us as authentically as he was present to them. The truth of this audacious faith hangs on the reality of Spirit.

But what is this Spirit that Jesus passes on and how is it experienced? The word *Spirit* is extremely elusive. Although it cannot be completely pinned down, its implications can be explored. Geoffrey Lampe says that

> [Spirit] is one of those "bridge" words which express the idea of God's outreach towards, and contact with, the created world...[it speaks] of God directing his thought towards his creation, purposing, willing, bringing into being, sustaining, guiding the cosmos and everything within it.[17]

In general, Spirit signifies the immanent presence of God to creation. But Spirit is more concretely grounded than that. It is an image taken from the experiences of breathing and wind. In Genesis, the passionate God breathes his breath into the clay human shape. The result is life; and the implication is that every inhalation of the human is the exhalation of the divine. God is not a distant reality, but as near and intimate as breath. In passing on the Spirit, Jesus performs the same act (John 20:22). He breathes on his disciples and tells them they are receiving the Holy Spirit. To talk about the Spirit of God is to indicate a presence as necessary, as subtle, and as sustaining as breath.

Spirit as breath suggests God's ubiquitous, permanent, life-supporting presence to creation. But God's involvement with creation is not confined to mere maintenance. Spirit as a steady divine influence is complemented by Spirit as an explosive divine outbreak of love, judgment, and transformation. Quiet breathing becomes a driving wind. Spirit not only upholds at all times; it especially inspires at crucial times.

It is best to talk about these special times as "break outs" rather than "break ins," because they are specifications of a presence that is already there and not intrusions of an absent power. It is these special times that we most often interpret as advents of the Spirit. We take breathing for granted; wind catches our attention.

Spirit, therefore, signifies the sustaining and transforming presence of God. This dynamic presence suffuses all creation. But it is not a reality that is directly known. It is only known by the effects it is producing in human life. The divine is not nakedly apprehended, but intuited by what it is making happen. Said in another way, God is co-known as the ultimate source and catalyst of certain experiences that have many other causal factors.

In any concatenation of events, there are many proximate players. These players are easily observed, and most of what goes on can be attributed to their agency. But, in some events, the proximate players become responsive to an ultimate author. What happens is not only the result of the energies of the proximate players, but of a larger creative energy which is working through them. When the ultimate author of the event is discerned amid the fury of the proximate players, we say, "The Spirit is present." To say this entails an act of discernment. Discernment is difficult business; but there is no other way to uncover and acknowledge the divine that is intimately involved in the human.

The necessity of discernment to proclaim the presence of the Spirit is seen from an episode in the Gospel of Matthew (12:22–37). Jesus cures a blind and dumb demoniac. Everyone is amazed, but no one is quite sure what to make of it. The people have questions. "Can this be the Son of David?" The Pharisees offer an interpretation. "It is only by Beelzebub, the Prince of Demons, that he casts out demons." Jesus offers an alternate understanding. "If it is by the Spirit of God that I cast out demons, then the Kingdom of God has come among you."

No one disputes that a healing has occurred. The quarrel is over the interpretation. Is the ultimate source and catalyst of the healing God or Satan? If the experience is discerned as permeated by divine influence, then Spirit is the image used to express and convey that conviction. Spirit is introduced into the conversation as the truest and fullest appraisal of what happened in the experience.

During the life of Jesus, he interpreted his own activity and people interpreted their experiences of him as Spirit-created. They did this because through him the peace and power of God entered human life. The Spirit Jesus leaves his friends is this same Spirit of God precisely as he specified it.

As James Dunn puts it, Jesus is the personality of the Spirit.[18] In another image, Jesus is the signature of the Spirit. The invisible, immanent presence of God gains visibility and definition in Jesus. It is no longer merely the Spirit of God. That is too vague a designation. Neither is it the Spirit of the God who "delivered Israel out of the house of bondage," the Spirit of God as specified by the Exodus-covenant experience. It is the Spirit that burst forth in the life, death, and resurrection of Jesus. In Trinitarian language, it is the Spirit of the Father and the Son.

The presence of the Spirit of Jesus among his followers is known in precisely the same way as the presence of the Spirit of God was known in Jesus, with one major change: the physical mediation of Jesus of Nazareth is replaced by his followers. Spirit is no longer an interpretive image for the depth of encounters with Jesus of Nazareth; but an image to interpret the depth of encounters among Christians.

As once Jesus mediated the Spirit to his followers, now they mediate the Spirit to one another and to all who come in contact with them. In and through experiences with the followers of Jesus, life is sustained and transformed not only by human ingenuity and creativity, but by the ultimate Mystery of life itself. The precise way of sustaining and transforming is indebted to Jesus who sustained and transformed life in a particular way. This is the experience of Spirit; and when it happens, Christians often express its reality by saying, "Christ is present!"

This new mediation is captured in the "great condition" that the Johannine Christ places on his continuing presence. He promises his friends another Paraclete "to be with you forever" (John 14:16); that the Father will love them and that he will love them and reveal himself to them (John 14:21); that he and the Father will make their dwelling place with them (John 14:23–24). But all these promises of continued presence are on the condition that they keep Jesus' commandments. In the Johannine literature, Jesus' words and commandments are summarized as "love one another as I have loved you."

But this condition should not be looked on as an automatic codicil. If Jesus' friends love one another, then Christ magically appears as a bonus. Rather their love for one another activates his presence. But it is a presence that is doubly mediated. First, it is mediated through the disciples and their effort to love one another. This effort at love discerns a divine encouragement, a greater Mystery that initiated the effort and accompanies it as it proceeds. This divine lure and assistance is the Spirit.

But it is not just *any* Spirit of *any* God. It is the Spirit of the God of Jesus and therefore carries the divine gift and demand that came to expression in the life, death, and resurrection of Jesus of Nazareth. This forms the second mediation. Through the disciples and through the Spirit, Jesus Christ is present. This image of "bequeathing the Spirit" is an interpretation of the crucial experience of the early Church—the simultaneous loss and presence of Jesus Christ.

We are now close to the heart of our reflections. With the miracle of birth, we enter into inescapable relationships with other people and God. The relationship with God is mediated through the other people; and once it is articulated and inhabited, it redounds back on them. But this living relationship with God can be neglected. Consciousness can be narrowed to the immediately observable.[19] The proximate players can overshadow the ultimate author.

This was not the case with Jesus. Jesus was a proximate player completely in accord with the ultimate author. When he was with people, he was the catalyst that brought the living relationship to God into the minds and hearts of people with both passion and precision. It is this conscious activation of the living relationship with God that is the center of Christian reality.

The Body of Christ

The Johannine image of bequeathing the Spirit is a natural companion of the Pauline image of the Church as the Body of Christ. In fact, in chapter twelve of First Corinthians, Paul smoothly connects Jesus, the Spirit, and the Church as the Body of Christ. The Spirit is discerned in believers because it urges them to cry, "Jesus is Lord!" and never "Cursed be Jesus!" It is also this Spirit which is the source of their many gifts and binds them into one body. "In the one Spirit we were all baptized into one body—Jews or Greeks, slaves or free—and we were all made to drink of one Spirit" (12:13).

"Body of Christ" is a phrase that is found often in the letters of Paul. D. E. H. Whiteley points out four different meanings for this phrase—the body of Christ in his earthly

life, the Resurrected Body of Christ, the Church, and the Eucharistic body.[20] These four realities are closely connected but
should not be collapsed into one another. Initially, "Body of
Christ" refers literally and really to the earthly and resurrected
body of Jesus. It refers metaphorically and really to the Church
and the Eucharist. Our concern is with one of the meanings it
conveys when it is metaphorically applied to the people who
are the Church.[21]

As an image for the deepest identity of the Church, "Body
of Christ" is rich in meanings. These multiple meanings are
brought out in interaction with different social situations. In
Corinth, the problem was that the diverse gifts of the community were creating disunity. Jealousy, rivalry, and factionalism
were resulting from the fact that one had the gift of prophecy;
another, the gift of tongues; another, the gift of healing; and so
on. The gifts were competing with one another, not cooperat-
ing.

In this situation, the metaphor of the Body of Christ becomes a call to harmony, to allow the diversity to become con-
tribution and not division. The basic metaphor is spelled out
in terms of eyes, feet, head, hands, and ears—all working together. None of them can claim to be autonomous. Each needs
the other to be whole. The meaning pulled from the Body of
Christ in interaction with the conflicts at Corinth is that our
unique gifts must unite us and not pull us apart.

But at Colossae, the situation was different. The people
were worshiping elemental cosmic spirits that ruled the world.
Between God and humankind there were a galaxy of mediators—"thrones or dominions or rulers or powers" (Colossians
1:16). These powers had to be appeased if life was to be secure
and productive. Jesus Christ was imaged as one of these powers, one who would give protection if properly placated.

In response to this situation, the "Body of Christ" image
is developed in a different direction. At Corinth, the head was

just one more member. At Colossae, Christ becomes the Head and the people are the Body. As Head, Christ has the fullness of authority and can guarantee the Body freedom from the cosmic spirits. There is no need to grovel before them, for as Church we are members of the Body whose Head is Christ. This Head has won a victory over the powers and principalities of the world. In the conflictual world of Colossae, the image is played out differently than in the conflictual world of Corinth.

Different conflicts elicit different meanings from the same image. The conflict we are considering is the loss of the physical presence of Jesus of Nazareth. It is a conflict, because his physical presence is the precondition for triggering the salvific experience of God. Without this presence, the salvific experience may disappear.

In this situation, to call the people the Body of Christ is to say that their physical presence to one another functions as Jesus' physical presence did when he walked the earth. Although he is gone, the salvific experience he precipitated is still possible. The people who are the Church now mediate to one another what Jesus once mediated to them. When this happens, they become the Body of Christ, the visible offer of God's salvific love.

This is what Romano Guardini meant in the first quote that opened this chapter about the Church making Christ contemporary. We live after Jesus Christ, but not without him. He is present wherever and whenever the God he revealed is sustaining and transforming human life. This God of Jesus needs but, paradoxically, never forces flesh. The divine seeks free people to freely give themselves. No hirelings, only daughters and sons.

The preeminent son, Jesus, opened himself to this divine reality and it flowed through him. His followers attempt the same openness and the same mediation. That is their ultimate identity; and when they are faithful to it, they are living in his Spirit and functioning as his Body. In Christian shorthand, they are making the event of Jesus Christ contemporaneous to each generation.

Edward Schillebeeckx opens *Christ: The Experience of Jesus As Lord* with, "It began with an encounter."[22] Our insistence is that what began as an encounter continues as an encounter. The original event of Jesus Christ was an interpersonal meeting of Jesus of Nazareth with other people. This encounter penetrated to their core persons, their relationship to ultimate reality, and restructured this reality salvifically. Through his human love, divine love entered and transformed the lives of people. In this experience, people recognized the presence of God; and they named the experience Spirit.

Although this Jesus of Nazareth now lives in the far reaches of God as the Risen Lord, the salvific experience that he made possible continues.[23] We acknowledge that its the ultimate author of this experience is his Spirit and that we are functioning as his Body. Through our human love for one another, inspired and supported by the Spirit of Jesus, we initiate one another into a relationship with that Ultimate Love which Jesus revealed.

When this happens, the event of Jesus Christ occurs, not in the original way, but in a way dependent upon yet different from those long-ago encounters. Therefore, access to the event of Jesus Christ is through our Spirit-suffused love for one another that transforms us into the Body of Christ.

The Memory of Jesus

No Christian pondering can go on for long without the sobering subject of sin. Things go wrong. The Spirit may blow where it will, and unpredictability may be part of God's gracious surprise. But there is also a question of which Spirit is blowing.

The perennial concern of Christian faith is how to test the Spirit. How can we be sure it is the Spirit of Jesus which prompts us? How do we know we are handing on the authentic revelation? As Karl Barth pointed out, the New Testament uses the same word for Judas "handing over" Jesus and for Christians "handing over" to one another their tradition.[24]

This problem of discerning the authentic Spirit was central to the early Church. Paul mentions it in one of his earliest letters. "Do not quench the Spirit. Do not despise the words of prophets, but test everything; hold fast to what is good, abstain from every form of evil" (1 Thessalonians 5:19–22).

The test of the Spirit that Paul developed had three main features.[25] Was the present activity attributed to the inspiration of the Spirit in continuity with the founding gospel traditions, did it manifest love, and was it for the benefit of others? These criteria are indebted to the memory of the event of Jesus Christ. It was this event that revealed the love of God and made possible an other-centered life. "The most profound safeguard which Paul offers against enthusiasm is the touchstone of Christ—the character of his ministry as testified in the gospel."[26] If there is to be contemporary access to the event of Jesus Christ, it is not enough to encounter people vivified by his Spirit. These people must also be in dialogue with his Memory.

The classic role for the Memory of Jesus has been as a critical corrective for Spirit. It has been called in to check the excesses of spiritual experiences. From a Christian viewpoint, spiritual experience is always in danger of breaking our life-giving bonds with the interpersonal world and setting us free to soar into private, ecstatic states. The Spirit lifts us out of the human circle and we begin to prefer this "disengaged" feeling. We wait and pray for these "escape moments" and tend to disdain the earth that holds us down. We relish the emotional highs and have little energy or interest in the ordinary. Any belief that does not bring with it the "thrill and feel of the Spirit," we suspect or discard.

In spiritual excess, "Praise the Lord!" is on our lips but forgotten is "Not everyone who says, 'Lord! Lord!' enters the kingdom of God." As Paul seemed to suggest, these experiences may take us to the seventh heaven, but they seldom seem to visit the cross of Christ. Their connection with other-centered love is weak. The ongoing, concrete demands of charitable living are drudgery compared to this spiritual excitement, and are soon neglected. Rational analysis is shunned as "killing the Spirit" and practical planning avoided because it shows a "lack of trust in God." Martin Luther mocked it well: "These people have swallowed the Holy Spirit, feathers and all."

But the question is "Just what have they swallowed?" The experience seems to arrive unaided by human love and often departs without inspiring human love. It is doubtful whether this type of experience should be called Spirit-created. The reason for this hesitancy is the Memory of Jesus. When we recall his life, death, and resurrection, we begin to question whether we should attribute to the inspiration of God any experience so isolated in its origins and so confined in its effects. Are these experiences authored by the Spirit of Jesus? Or are these experiences alien to the Spirit of Jesus? The only way these crucial questions can be answered is to consult the Memory of the Spirit-Giver.

But the Memory of Jesus does more than confront the excesses of spiritual experience. It also questions the arrogance of spiritual possession. "We have the Spirit," we say, as if it were a bird in a cage of our making. "Jesus promised it would be with us forever," we say, like a greedy nephew at the reading of a rich uncle's will. We complacently assume the Spirit is ours. We do not point to a life of love grounded in God to support this belief. We prefer to take it "on faith," which is comfortably defined as "beyond experience." The danger of spiritual enthusiasm often appears on the periphery of the people who are the Church. The larger danger of spirit possession is as a temptation at the center. It is the seduction of those in authority.

Now there is a great deal of truth in holding tightly to Jesus' promise that the Spirit would accompany us. We must trust in the presence of the Spirit, even when the experiences that validate that presence are not there. But this truth turns treacherous when we smugly use it to claim possession of the Spirit, even though the love, justice, and peace which are signs of that presence are nowhere to be found.

It is one thing to trust in the Spirit when the Spirit appears absent. This attitude understands the Spirit as the free gift of God and is receptive to its comings and goings. But it is another thing to claim the Spirit without openness to the experiences the Spirit generates, to lightly boast of its presence in the face of lovelessness, apathy, and envy. This attitude has taken the Spirit hostage.

Spirit possession is a theology of election gone sour. A Church which claims the Spirit as a prerogative begins to glory in itself, emphasize its privileged status, and blur the distinction between itself and Jesus Christ. In this situation, it is time for the Memory of Jesus. Yves Congar, who strongly emphasized the Spirit as the animating life force of the Church, subtly pointed to this aberration. "The Church's fidelity to her Lord demands not only that she listen to him within herself, in her own conscience, but also as the voice of Another, her Master."[27] Without the memory of the Master, we make ourselves the master and put the Spirit at the service of our self-aggrandizement. An important task of the Memory of Jesus is to keep his followers from an infatuation with spiritual highs and from a self-righteous posturing that will not brook criticism.

It has often been charged that Memory has done this job too well. If there can be an excess of Spirit, there can also be an excess of Memory. The dominance of Memory begins with praising the past as a time of extraordinary events. There was a time, the days and nights of Jesus of Nazareth, when the presence of God was immediate and tangible. These past events of which Jesus was the center were recorded, and we must be rigorously faithful to them. We must preserve these traditions intact and jealously guard them from error. Northrop Frye has slyly remarked: "In the post biblical period both Christianity and Judaism seem to have accepted the principle that the age of prophesy had ceased, and to have accepted it with a good deal of relief."[28] The wild ways of the Spirit give way to trustworthy truths taken from the golden age of revelation, rationally defended and authoritatively passed on.

With Memory so enshrined, present religious experience is ignored or, at best, highly suspect. This opens the way for authoritarian religion at its worst. Since we cannot trust any intimation of God garnered from our experience, we must blindly believe the witnesses of the past. More particularly, we must submit to the authoritative interpretations of what those witnesses had to say.

There is no possibility of dissent for we have no other access to the Divine except through their witness. We believe on the word of another; and we construct edifices of argument to convince ourselves that these others are trustworthy. We console ourselves with the words of the Johannine Christ to the doubting Thomas. Thomas was granted every believer's fantasy. He fingered the wounds of the Risen Christ and physically bolstered his sagging faith. But he is not blessed. It is we who are blessed, the ones who believe and do not see.

But this will not get us through the winters of our doubt and discontent. If the day arrives when the past is not solid certainty, we can base our lives on but just someone else's truth. Franz Kafka caught the tone of that day in a brief parable.

They were offered the choice between becoming kings
or the couriers of kings. The way children would, they
all wanted to be couriers. Therefore there are only couriers who hurry about the world, shouting to each
other—since there are no kings—messages that have
become meaningless. They would like to put an end to
this miserable life of theirs but they dare not because
of their oaths of service.[29]

When we retain the message of the King but lose the feel for
his presence, the passion of religious mission turns to dull obligation.

Christian faith points to certain events of the past as extraordinary and special. No one living today was present at them.
And, if the reports are to be believed, the majority of people
who were fortunate enough (Christian nostalgia) to be present
at these events missed their revelatory impact. But the specialness
of the past should not usurp the specialness of the present. The
life and times of Jesus and the early Church may have been
bursting with Spirit, but we are not bereft of it. The same Spirit
that suffused the life of Jesus in a preeminent way, and through
him the disciples, prophets, and mystics of the Christian tradition, is also at work in the life of the ordinary believer of today.

The Memory of Jesus records a time of the intensification
of the Spirit. But this does not overshadow or discount less
intense experiences of the same Spirit. In fact, it is the present
experience of the Spirit, however weak or powerful, which
makes it possible for the contemporary believer to recognize
the fullness of Spirit in the Memory of Jesus.

In the excesses and pretensions of the Spirit, we look to
the Memory of Jesus for direction and perspective. But when
Memory threatens to alienate us from the depth of the present,
we look to the Spirit to bring us life. Spirit and Memory are
critical correctives.[30] The enduring adventure of Christian faith

is to keep them in creative tension with one another. Which brings us by a circuitous route back to that living room in a home on the northwest side of Chicago.

The woman holds the witness to the original event of Jesus Christ and wants to insert it into the discussion. The man is "into" the conversation among the people and wants no interference from the Bible. As might be expected, both have a piece of the action.

The most positive interpretation of the man's closing the Bible is that he is sensitive to the sustaining and transforming of life that is happening in the group and through the group in the parish. He sees the introduction of the biblical witness as shifting attention from the present to the past. Christ is present now. The experience of Spirit, which is Jesus' legacy, is happening among his latest band of followers. With this perspective, the dilemma he will eventually run into is how to discern the Spirit's impulse. When this happens, he might turn to the woman with the Bible with less irritation.

The most positive interpretation of the Bible-quoting woman is that she is consulting the Memory of Jesus in order to better discern the dynamics of the present. She is not trying to distract from the group processes and the necessary decisions that have to be made; she is trying to focus those processes and clarify the real terms of the decision. She might be afraid that the group will go "off on its own" and analyze and plan without the illumination that comes from the Jesus story. If it does that, the group might not hear the ultimate author in the noise of the proximate players. She is trying to give the group "ears" or, in another metaphor, "eyes."

With this perspective, the dilemma she will eventually run into is what these words from the past have to do with the dynamics of the present situation. When this happens, she might turn to the man who just turned to her and ask, "What were you saying about the presence of Christ?"

An Experience of Spirit: A Summary

It is people, always people, interacting with the world and other people. But it is never only people. There is always More, a crucial but often overlooked More. This More is the ultimate Mystery of life that is the permeating context of the interacting people. This ultimate Mystery both sustains the human adventure and transforms it. We name this sustainer and transformer Spirit.

Though the Spirit is the ultimate author of life itself, the ultimate authorship never excludes the proximate players. In fact, it is the proximate players, the people themselves, who speak of the Spirit's influence or who neglect to mention it. A religious appreciation of the human condition locks the divine and human spirit, the ultimate author and proximate players, in a living relationship.

Jesus was also a proximate player of immense vitality. When people were with him, life was sustained with such a love and transformed with such a passion that the only adequate interpretation was that the "Spirit of God was upon him." This Spirit that worked through him during his life sustained him through the terrors of death and transformed him into a new existence.

Jesus now lives in the unimaginable transcendence of God which John had the nerve to imagine as a mansion with many rooms and Jesus as a housekeeper, gone on ahead, to ready the place for our arrival.

For the early Church, the ascension of Jesus meant that he had taken on a new role. The imagery for this new role was that he "sat at the right hand of the Father." The implication is that everything that the Father does is now channeled through Jesus, the Son. The preeminent activity of the Father is the sending of Spirit. Jesus is now part of that commissioning. During Jesus' earthly life, the Father sends the Spirit, which descends upon Jesus and empowers him to be the Son. But, with the ascension, Jesus is linked so closely to God that he moves from being the recipient of the Spirit to being the co-sender of the Spirit.

The experience of Spirit now happens among the ones whom Jesus left behind, but did not leave orphans. The inheritance that Jesus left his brothers and sisters was the Spirit. This Spirit is the animating energy of their interaction with one another; and it effects what Jesus' earthly presence once brought about. In this sense, the people become the Body of Christ, the current mediation of the event that happened in and through Jesus of Nazareth.

The contemporary people who are the Body of Christ do not replace Jesus, the first Body of Christ; rather they mediate his presence to one another and the world in which they live. The Spirit that is sent by the Risen Lord and which empowers the people to be the Body of Christ is bringing about what it brought about in the earthly life of Jesus. Therefore, the Memory of Jesus is necessary to discern the present activity of the Spirit. This exploration suggests that the deepest identity of the Christian Church is that they are a people of Spirit and Memory.

For Further Reflection

1. Some thinkers have compared the transmission of the story of Jesus Christ from generation to generation as a kind of "contagion," that the reality Jesus unleashed into the world spreads like a disease. Each person who is exposed becomes, in turn, a carrier to other people. What is your view of this metaphor in light of the information in this chapter?

2. What do you think is the next moment in the conversation between the woman who opened the Bible to find Jesus and the man who flipped it shut in the name of Christ?

How do these two reflect both the presence and absence of Jesus?
3. Read the following story. How does it reflect the resistance of human love? How does it reflect the persistence of divine love? How might you retell this story in contemporary terms?

⚜

The Old Woman and the Spider

The Ganges was calm. Peace was upon the waters as the young girl walked the banks of the river. Her thoughts were the thoughts of youth. Who would she marry? What would she do? How many children would she have? Would she be rich and have servants? Ahead of her she noticed an old woman. She was dressed in a beautiful sari and her face was radiant. Next to her, the Ganges appeared a troubled river.

As the young woman approached her, the old woman suddenly bent over some branches that had washed into shore. Her hand moved among the branches; then she quickly pulled it out. When the young woman was close enough, she saw what was happening. A spider had impaled itself on a thorn and the woman was trying to free it. But every time she attempted to lift the spider off, he bit her. She would remove her hand, suck the poisonous blood from her finger, and try again.

The young woman watched her for a while and spoke. "Old woman, what foolishness is this? Leave the spider to its fate. Every time you try to help it, it repays you with a bite."

The old woman smiled. "The spider's nature is to bite. Mine is to save. Will I lose myself on the banks of this sacred river?"

The younger woman said nothing, but her face showed that she was puzzled. In her heart the old woman hoped that her smile was not lost on the young one.

Chapter Two

The Creations of the People of Spirit and Memory

The classic event for the Christian is the religious event of God's self-manifestation in the person Jesus the Christ: an event that happened, happens, and will happen.[1]

DAVID TRACY

*T*he heart of Christian faith is this salvific experience which we have of Spirit. There is an experiential continuity between what Jesus made happen and what happens among his followers. The vitality of this experience has generated immense creative activity. This central animating experience is the source of the many creations of the people of Spirit and Memory. Their rich and varied traditions flow from this experience and lead back to it. We have identified an experience of Spirit. In this chapter, we will explore its manifold expressions.

The Voices

The time is 1954. The place is Chicago. The boy is thirteen. He belongs to the people of Spirit and Memory. But the people of Spirit and Memory have journeyed far—spatially, temporally, and developmentally—since the inaugural events of first-century Palestine.

The boy is wearing a cassock, sash, surplice, and cape. He is kneeling in a Gothic church before a monstrance. At the center of the monstrance is a consecrated host. The boy has been told since childhood that Christ lives in this host. He is not especially pious; but he believes it. Whatever doubts he had were allayed by a heavy classroom discussion on transubstantiation. The idea was just far enough beyond his intellectual abilities to convince him.

This kneeling boy contemplating the host as a sacred object seems a far cry from the original eucharistic setting of eating and drinking with Jesus. The people of Spirit and Memory have been journeying through time and space and living off the land.

Many things have changed; fewer things have remained the same. Within the Christian tradition, many have deplored this process of development and adaptation. For them, every change was smacked with betrayal. Others have welcomed development. For them, change is a sign of vitality. Both groups, from time to time, have misgivings about their strong stances; but they seldom share these qualms with each other.

This faded photo from 1954 is itself a lesson in historical development. The clothes the boy is wearing were fashionable centuries earlier in Western Europe. The architecture that surrounds him was inspired by the towering spirituality of the Middle Ages. The particular form of piety he is practicing— exposition of the Blessed Sacrament and praying before it— started around the thirteenth century.

The boy is one of a long series of altar boys who will kneel before the Blessed Sacrament on this day. They work in half-hour shifts; two at a time. It is part of the Forty Hours Devotion. The boy knows the routine—kneel fifteen minutes, sit fifteen minutes. He has a prayer book, which he reads and ponders; then his mind wanders. Although he tries hard, he has always had trouble with "paying attention."

His knees were hurting and he was checking his watch to see if it was time to sit when the host, without saying a word, spoke to him.

"I'm not just a host, you know."

The boy sat immediately. To put it mildly, he was discombobulated. But every time he looked at the monstrance the same wordless words came to him.

"I'm not just a host, you know."

He looked over at his fellow server. This boy, also thirteen, was famous for his ears. They were enormous jug handles; and with immense concentration and teeth grinding he was able to slide them noticeably back and forth on the side of his head. As Nelson Algren was fond of saying, "Talent can spring up anywhere."

The boy's world got "mysteriouser and mysteriouser." On the way home, everything talked to him. Two old ladies on the street addressed him without saying a word, "We're not just two old ladies, you know." The trees felt compelled to repeat the message; so did the sky. The boy was dizzy with all this unsolicited companionship.

It was the "you know" at the end of all these unexpected outbursts of communication from all these normally silent realities that most shocked the boy. The fact is he had not known. Until that day everything was what it was and nothing more. Never again was this to be the case. Something had happened to the structure of his awareness. It had been broken and recast to include more of what was. Everything was more than it seemed; everything opened onto something greater.

And it was the something greater that whispered the message. It was as if the boy had been let in on a great secret. So, in the secrecy of his soul, he gave the day a name. He called it the Day of the Haloes. For now he knew the radiance of each person.

⋅⊹&⊹⋅

The Boy in Context

Of course, the boy grew up and in a rage of sophistication rejected the happenings of that day. From the liberated vantage point of young adulthood, it seemed to him to be ghetto Catholicism at its narrowest. How could he trust voiceless communications from a host and then from the entire world? Was not this the wish fulfillment of a mind seduced by magic? He must have been a lonely boy and his own loneliness spoke to him from the host. In his heart, he knew this was not true, but at least it was understandable.

The boy-turned-man moved from piety to people. Did not Jesus switch the locale of the sacred from the temple to the person? He abandoned the church buildings, both physically and spiritually. He traded the dimly lit spaces where hosts spoke in solitude for the world of "I-Thou" encounters and social conflicts.

A theology accompanied him on his journey. God was present in people, not things; in the events of history, not in buildings. What counted was bread in people's mouths, not hosts in monstrances.

It was in his early thirties that the boy-turned-man read a passage from Teilhard de Chardin about a man kneeling before the Eucharist.

Thus in the midst of a great sigh suggestive both of an awakening and of a plaint the flow of whiteness enveloped me, passed beyond me, overran everything. At the same time everything, though drowned in this whiteness, preserved its own proper shape, its own autonomous movement; for the whiteness did not efface the features or change the nature of anything, but penetrated objects at the core of their being, at a level more profound even than their own life. It was as though a milky brightness were illuminating the universe from within, and everything were fashioned of the same kind of translucent flesh.[2]

The boy-turned-man knew what the writer was talking about. It was not the same as his experience of long ago. There was no paradoxical communication without words. The experience was expressed in visual terms. But the result was very much the same—the sense of an inner radiance which etched everything in its unmistakable uniqueness. Nothing was just anything. Everything was more than it seemed. The opaque world became translucent.

The boy-turned-man was still unsure about the day the host, without speaking, spoke. He could not wrap his critical mind around it. But even though he could not comprehend what happened, he was more ready to accept it. The experience had left a mark on him and he might as well acknowledge it.

Every time he tried to reduce the reality of another person (and he tried it often) something happened; and the communication inevitably came through: "I'm more than just a person who wriggles their ears, you know." Whenever this happened, the boy-turned-man was startled by the "you know." He knew but yet he did not know. He kept forgetting; and each time he was reminded, the new experience connected with the old ones to deepen his awareness.

The Spirit As Energy Center

The previous chapter stressed that the people of Spirit and Memory were constituted by a living relationship with God. The experience of this relationship was inaugurated and definitively enacted in the event of Jesus Christ. But it is not a relationship or an experience that is lost in the onward rush of time and history.

Even though Jesus is not with us the way he once was, the experience of this relationship with us and his Father continues in the Church. This living relationship with divine reality and the experience of Spirit is the "energy center" of Christian faith.

This energy center releases the creative powers of people. Whenever the experience of Spirit, as David Tracy suggests, "happened, happens, and will happen," there is a rich and diversified human response. The inrush of divine reality sets people rushing off in many directions. In the throes and wake of this experience, people create; and the sum of their creations form the Christian tradition. All the creations, or in a more majestic phrase, "the monuments," of the tradition flow from this experienced relationship to God and are meant to continually refer back to it. The divine which originates the creativity ultimately claims it.

But this dynamic, emerging from and returning to the experience of God, is not always easy to trace. Many liturgical, doctrinal, ecclesiastical, and political developments of Christian history seem to have little to do with the living relationship to God. Yet when the historical spadework is done, what often turns up is a theological rationale for its development, an attempt to connect it to the foundational revelation. The development may have been generated by personal or political self-interest and later made presentable with theology. But even if in a given instance of self-interest this was the case, the instinct that guides all creations of the people of Spirit and Memory was at work. Every development must be related—somehow—to the experience of Spirit.

The creations of the people of Spirit and Memory defy neat categories. Christian history is not a model of progressive and orderly development. It is a sprawling chronicle of a people who are energized by their living relationship to God and who are creating multiple responses to their diverse environments. They were "productively perverse."

Their efforts range from the gospels of Jesus Christ to the legends of the saints; from the eucharistic meal to a long-forgotten burial custom of fourth-century Italy; from the theological synthesis of Thomas Aquinas to the countless sermons that died in mid-sentence; from the music of Palestrina and the art of Michelangelo to the tavern ditties spruced up for church services and the rosy-cheeked Christs of weepy piety. Any tradition as old as Christianity is bound to be a motley mix of motley people parading the motley work of their hands.

Our opening scene of a Catholic boy kneeling before the Blessed Sacrament in 1954 is a snapshot of one moment in the life of this pilgrim people. To be born into or to convert into a religious tradition is to encounter its myriad creations. There is no direct access to the experience of Spirit. What a person initially "bumps up against" are the structures, ethics, beliefs, theology, spiritual practices, myth, and ritual of the religious people to which he or she belongs. The Church is not just a people of Spirit and Memory, but a historical people who have undergone the struggles of time and space and have a storehouse of created traditions. When these created traditions are functioning properly, they seduce believers into the living relationship with God.

The boy cannot escape time. He cannot leapfrog back to Christ to find a more palatable mediation of God. Initially, we all take what we get; and in time we change what we have received in ways we think are more appropriate. In doing so, we insist that the generation after us initially take what they get.

In chapter one, we focused on the people of Spirit and Memory. In this chapter we focus on the traditions the people have generated. We will use the ambiguous experience of the boy and the ambiguous reflections of the boy-turned-man as a touchstone.

The Experience of Spirit: Embodied in Myth and Ritual

Although there may be no method to the madness of how the Christian tradition developed, there are priorities. The most prized creations of the Christian tradition are its core myth and ritual. The core myth is the life, death, and resurrection of Jesus Christ which is embodied in the four gospels; the core ritual is the eucharistic eating and drinking together that he initiated.

In the course of Christian history, this myth and ritual was elaborated into six other rituals with readings from the core myth and the other books of Scripture. This became known as Word and Sacrament and formed the center of the Christian tradition. The Protestant reformation is often analyzed, in hindsight, as the "effective but not total" separation of Word and Sacrament. Generally speaking, the Protestants took the book and the Catholics took the sacraments. The result is that both groups were impoverished.

The core myth and ritual of Christianity is prized because it is the primary expression of the salvific experience triggered by Jesus, the experience known as Spirit.[3] Myth and ritual are not secondary reflections upon the experience; they are the very embodiment of the experience. They are the privileged creations that carry the experience through time and history and make it available to each new generation.

This is what is meant by saying that the core myth and

ritual are symbolic. When people participate in them with receptivity and openness, they can move through the words, gestures, and objects into the reality of God. This myth and ritual was generated by the experience of God and so is capable of communicating that experience. This capacity to put the participant into the living relationship to God that was revealed in Jesus Christ is signified by calling the myth the Word of God and the ritual elements the body and blood of Christ.

The Catholic boy in the story that opened our reflections is participating in a historical offshoot of the core ritual. He has been baptized; and so, in one understanding of baptism, he has been formally initiated into the living relationship to God. He has also been socialized into the Catholic, Christian tradition. He has been exposed to the theological understanding of the Real Presence of Christ in the Eucharist and has found it persuasive. So he is an open, if somewhat distracted, adorer of Christ.

What happens to this boy is that through no effort of his own (at least as far as he knows) this living relationship to God enters his mind and heart. He becomes conscious of the transparency of all things to their divine grounding. The mediation of this awareness came through one of the historical developments—Hours of Adoration—connected with the core ritual of Eucharist.

This is not a "squeaky clean" example of how participation in the core myth and ritual of Christian religion puts one in contact with the founding salvific experience. First, the myth dimension is missing during the experience. The boy knows the story of Jesus but that knowledge is not an active component of the experience.

Second, it is not really the core ritual but a development which is significantly different from original intentionality of the ritual. The original table fellowship was a meal which involved active engagement with actual others and symbolized the advent of God's reign. In this paraliturgical activity, the interaction is between the individual and the holy object. It begins with pondering and wandering and ends in encounter. It would seem that the only hope of continuity through the labyrinth of historical development is the dynamics of the underlying experience.

But just what does the boy experience? He becomes aware of the host, his fellow server, the old women, and everything else in a new way. He perceives them in relationship to a fullness of reality which they are capable of revealing.

In his reflections on the experience later in life, he is leery of what "actually went on." Although paradoxical language like "talking without words" is fully at home in his religious tradition and he feels this expresses what happened, his adult, secular self is skeptical.

What boy-turned-man is not skeptical about is the truth he has taken from the experience. He is convinced people are more than they seem. He struggles with this truth and tries to be faithful to its implications. When he is not, something happens which reminds him of the uniqueness of each person in relationship to the fullness of reality; and he learns again this easily forgotten truth and so reforms his response.

What can be said about this experience in relationship to the salvific experience which is expressed in the New Testament witness? It is partial and fragmentary, but important. It seems that one of the effects of Jesus' table fellowship with people was the growing conviction of their uniqueness. The ending of the Zacchaeus story states that he knows what it means to be a son of Abraham (Luke 19:9).

This signals the emergence of an identity to which he must be responsible. The boy's experience parallels this. He has a growing awareness of the unique reality that each person is, a uniqueness grounded in a transcendent otherness, a uniqueness that cannot be collapsed into the obvious and the observable.

He senses a call to respond to this uniqueness and not just the functional dimension of relationships. What he experienced is in continuity with the experience of Spirit.

But, as far as communicating anything like the fullness of the experience of Spirit, this event was only the merest whisper. But it seems that for most people, life is composed of whispers that gradually become a distinct voice. The rhetoric that the core myth and ritual of Christianity "re-presents" the reality and produces "repetitive"[4] and "dependent"[5] revelations assures us of the possibility, but it neglects the tentative and piecemeal actuality.

Receiving the salvific experience at the center of Christian faith is usually a gradual, diverse, and cumulative process of many contacts with its core myth and ritual. Appropriating this experience as the center of one's thinking and action is equally gradual, diverse, and cumulative. T. S. Eliot was correct in his observation that a tradition is only made one's own only with great labor.

The core myth and ritual of Christianity reflects the artistic dimension of the human person. For our purposes, the artist in each person appropriates reality by feeling its fullness. Feeling includes both cognitive appreciation and affective resonance and unites both in the deeper center of the responding person.[6] Feeling responses to divine-human interaction are usually initially expressed in imaginative forms. Imaginative forms—poetry, story, art, music—are capable of a fullness of expression, of bringing the totality of what was experienced to light. They are also capable of triggering feeling-responses in others.[7] They have powerful interactive potential.

This potential includes the feeling responses to reality that the people who created the imaginative form intended and feeling responses to reality of which they were not aware. Myth and ritual, as artistic forms, are multivalent and plurisignificant. They can evoke many feelings and many meanings.

Once, through myth and ritual, the living relationship to God has been experienced, other human processes take over. We "chew over" what has been experienced and tease out its implications for cognitive beliefs, ethical actions, and structural possibilities. But logically previous to this process is the experience, as the following story illustrates.

❧

The Teacher Who Never Explained

A story is told about a teacher who taught by poem, story, and art. He never explained the poems, stories, or art; he merely solicited responses of the students as they heard or viewed the art. This infuriated the students who were continually asking him what these works meant. One day the teacher put an apple on the desk. He asked the students what they saw. "An apple," was the wary response, sure they were being tricked. "Is anyone hungry?" asked the teacher. One young man was. "Do you want the apple?" "It looks delicious," said the young man. "Good," replied the teacher, "but first let me chew it up for you." Experience precedes reflection.

❧

The artist's response to art is often more art. When we hear the passion of Jesus Christ, the thinker in us may puzzle over God's seeming passivity in the face of evil. The artist in us may compose a poem on suffering, tell a story of courage, sing a song of sorrow, paint a picture of death. These responses, and many more, are within all of us. But the qualities and possibilities of the responses differ.

When the mind answers the experience mediated through the core myth and ritual, we move toward theology. When the imagination answers the experience mediated through the core myth and ritual, we move toward a new and contemporary embodiment of the experience. This new embodiment attempts to express what was found in the experience and evoke that in all others who come in contact with the imaginative work. Art and theology are complementary; but they have different ambitions.

The importance within a tradition of new, imaginative recastings of the foundational salvific experience can hardly be exaggerated. First, it is a sign that the core myth and ritual is working. In participating in the core myth and ritual, something is being experienced with enough depth and power to generate an imaginative response.

Word and Sacrament are the sun of Christian faith. When their inner energy is exploding outward, they produce the planets of Christian culture. When the art of a religious tradition becomes mundane or is gradually disappearing, it is a sign that the vital center is not communicating. On the other hand, when Christian-inspired art is flourishing, it is a sign that the core myth and ritual is functioning symbolically and initiating people into the experience known as Spirit. A Christian culture of poems, plays, novels, music, sculpture, and painting is not merely the take-it-or-leave-it periphery of the indispensable center of Bible and liturgy. It is a sign that Bible and liturgy are vibrant realities.

Second, the artistic creations of a tradition provide fresh access to the founding salvific experience. Since they are inspired by the living relationship to God expressed in the core myth and ritual, they have the possibility of evoking the felt-experience of that relationship. They are indebted to the privileged Scripture and liturgy and continue its communicative mission in new ways. Their role within the totality of the Christian tradition is to make the experience known as Spirit contemporary.

The sense of sin may not come through in reading Genesis Three; but it is overwhelming in Francois Mauriac's novels. We may become inured to the constant call for conversion in the Gospels; but it is immediate, real, and costly in the short stories of Flannery O'Connor. The emotional power of Jesus' presence might escape notice as we parse Matthew; but it will sweep us away in Zeffirelli's *Jesus of Nazareth* or Gibson's *The Passion of the Christ*.

In our boy, a poetic streak shows up. He calls his revelatory experience the "Day of the Haloes." He borrows what is all around him in the church—statues of saints with haloes—and suffuses it with personal meaning. This image then carries the experience in compressed form; and whenever he sees a halo (they are hard to come by these days), he will be reminded of the experience.

The boy also articulates the experience in more expository language; but this language will not function in the same way. The image is evocative code for the total impact of the experience. "Day of the Haloes" is not a metaphor for the ages. But it does exemplify the quiet imaginative way all of us who are not Shakespeare express and communicate our depth experiences.

Belief and Theology:
Expressions of the Experience of Spirit

The experience of Spirit expressed and communicated in Christian myth and ritual affects the total person. It is not geared merely to the mind or to the affections or to the will or to behavior. It addresses the centered self, the person as ultimately constituted.

Jesus called this centered self "heart" and made it the primary target of his ministry. As the Church entered the Hellenistic world, new terminology developed. *Soul* replaced *heart* and became the classic term for the primary arena of divine activity. If we could divest the term *soul* of its dualistic overtones and false competition with *body*, its more powerful meaning might emerge. Soul is the ultimate source of all human activity. It is the hidden, unifying center of the person.

When God stirs the soul and the soul responds, the soul speaks the experience. Mary's prayer in the Gospel of Luke says it explicitly: "My soul magnifies the Lord" (Luke 1:46). This initial language of religious experience has the qualities of immediacy, passion, abundance, and imagination. The language is rushing out of the experience, tumbling over itself in the effort to express what has happened.

But what has happened has been the immanent touch of a transcendent God. The experience is essentially ineffable. The soul cheerfully admits this; and then continues to bubble forth image after image. What happened is more than words can say; but we cannot stop saying words. Theologians often categorize this immediate, expressive activity as the first-order language of religion.

The mind, in a cooler moment, takes note of the soul's exuberance. The soul spoke out of abundance and produced a language of "prayerful explosion," a language designed to express and evoke. This language is rich in insight and feeling, but not precise.

The mind wants a clearer cognitive grasp of what happened in the experience. So it inhabits anew the first-order language and through it explores the living relationship to God. Through this activity it comes to some touchstone truths and states them in a first-order language of its own.

It is not always easy to distinguish the first-order language of religious experience and the first-order language of cognitive appropriation. Some biblical candidates might be: "Christ God was reconciling the world to himself" (2 Corinthians 5:19) or it is precisely in this that "God proves his love for us in that while we were still sinners Christ died for us" (Romans 5:8). Expressions like these try to deliver the cognitive content of the experience. They might be called the basic beliefs of faith.

Our Catholic boy has cognitively grasped his experience as "people are more than they seem" or "everything opens onto something larger." There was more in the experience than these phrases capture. But the nature of this type of activity is to articulate the experience in a summary phrase in order to clarify its meaning. This crystallizing of the experience makes it permanently available. The experience ends for the boy; but he carries with him the distilled truth. His phrasing of the experience is typically secular. God is intimated in the language, but not boldly present. He reflects the timidity of the modern mind concerning matters metaphysical.

Once the touchstone truths are in place, the mind begins to investigate these truths. This is the second-order language of theology. The religious experience is crystallized into basic beliefs, and the basic beliefs are explored. Faith seeks understanding.

The first type of mental activity called theology investigates the meaning and truth of the basic affirmations of faith. From this perspective, the history of theology within a religious tradition is the continual activity of conceptually penetrating and interrelating the distilled affirmations of religious experience. This activity is fueled by the development of human knowledge. The findings of science, psychology, sociology, biology, and philosophy dialogue with belief.

The basic affirmation that "God is at work in the world" finds different conceptualities in Aristotelian and Whiteheadean metaphysics. Petitionary prayer takes on new meaning in a Chardinian universe. The doctrine of creation unfolds slowly when it confronts the "big bang." Belief in life after death finds some unlikely allies in the mind-body debates of contemporary biology. The enigma of sin can receive a depth interpretation from psychoanalytic theory. The history of theology is an account of basic beliefs in dialogue with cultural knowledge.[8]

This mental activity is a drive toward intelligibility and coherence. It is running with the suggestion of the First Letter of Peter to give an account for the hope that is in you. This theological effort is extremely important. Without intelligibility, basic beliefs languish. It is not that they disappear. The Christian religious tradition is enormously retentive. Everything gets stored in the attic: very little is thrown out.

But the beliefs that are not accompanied by intelligent understanding cease to be influential in the decisions that make or break individual and social life. It is not that they are actively refuted; they are just passively not considered. Without a clue to their truth and meaning, they are often maddeningly relegated to the "mystery" of faith. But this is merely polite dismissal. The real word is not *mystery*, but *mystification*. Mystery occurs when the mind reaches its furthest exploration and lives in wonder. Mystification happens when the mind is paralyzed and lives in confusion. Theology which seeks intelligibility is not optional. It is essential to vital faith.

But the mind is infinitely agile. It does more than explore its kernelized affirmations. A second mental move attempts to extend the influence of the basic beliefs to all areas of human life. Most first-order faith statements have to do with the God-World relationship. They try to construe the flow of the ultimate relationship people experience. But this God-relationship cannot be isolated from all the other relationships that constitute the fabric of human existence. The religious relationship is the depth of personal, interpersonal, social, and ecological relationships.[9] As such, it attempts to influence how we perceive these realities. The theological activity that flows from ultimate affirmations instinctively moves to gather all realities "under its wings."

This is the integrating activity that is natural to all deeply religious people. If divine reality is the most important relationship of human life, should not all of life be apprehended from that perspective? So the mind works to construct an appreciation of everything within life from its foundational convictions about the Mystery of Life.

What does our relationship to God have to say about joining the military, sexual love, the distribution of wealth, fame, relationships with non-Christians, enemies, the exercise of authority, dietary laws, the way we worship, membership requirements, slavery, political systems, medical procedures, mental illness. This theological activity constructs a world in which to see properly the dynamics of every area of life. It results in endless "theologies of"—marriage, body, world, politics, and so on. At its best, this activity is the prelude to action.

This mental activity which is generated by the foundational religious experience is constantly interplaying with contemporary events. Time and history "throw up" new situations which faith immediately tries to comprehend from its unique perspective. How does faith see the problem of world hunger? What is the faith response to both capitalism and socialism? What is the place of technology when it is viewed from a faith perspective? What does faith have to say about the use of nuclear weapons? The Christian people at their best do not try to escape the conflicts and developments of each historical epoch. They attempt to create perspectives and responses out of their most foundational convictions.

The mind both explores the basic beliefs of faith and constructively extends their influence into the diversified concerns of human living. In a third move, the mind turns self-critical. It looks sympathetically, but unflinchingly, at its own religious formation. One of its faith affirmations concerns the depth of sin, and it knows that it is no exception to this contamination.

Theology attempts to raise consciousness about the processes of religion. How does religious experience and belief function in the life of the individual and society? The manifest objective of basic beliefs is to disclose the ultimate nature of the divine-human mystery. But the latent functioning of any given belief may be something completely different. Belief in life after death may state the truth about human destiny, but it can function to sap energies from the tasks of this life. That the Son of God died on the cross may be the supreme revelation of God, but it may also encourage a sick fascination with pain. The mind's passion for a "fullness of truth" demands that it becomes critical of the functioning of its own cherished beliefs.

This third type of mental activity focuses on the personal and social ecology of belief and theology. It is deeply suspicious and attempts to unmask false processes that may be operative in the espousal of belief and the construction of theology. An example from individual life might be a man who makes the cornerstone of his faith the belief, "The poor shall inherit the earth."

Suspicious minds ask why this statement has become so prominent. It may spy beneath this belief a convoluted process. These may people deeply desire wealth, but are impotent to achieve it. So they mask this impotence by espousing the opposite; and in this way secretly take revenge on those who have the riches they want. Their belief does not flow from the fullness of religious experience, but from distorted psychic processes.[10] The long-term effect of falsely grounded religious beliefs is the corrosion of the human spirit.

On the social level, this mental activity detects the ideological mechanisms in belief and theology. What is explicitly held because it is revelation may be implicitly reinforcing the prestige, power, and position of the group. After belief is stated and theology elaborated, the critical question is "Who wins?" If after a theology of salvation has been elaborated, the Catholic Church is more gloriously reigning than ever before, the critical mind becomes suspicious. If the end result of a theology of ministry is that everyone is the bishop's helper, the critical mind becomes suspicious. If when the Gospel is proclaimed the chests of people puff with pride at how good they are, the critical mind becomes suspicious. The question "Who wins?" tries to keep belief and theology honest and make them true servants of the experience of Spirit.

The multiple moves of the mind energized by religious experience are beyond charting. We have merely mentioned three. Our Catholic boy has tentatively engaged in these processes. At the time of the experience, he had a belief that "Christ is present in the Eucharist" and some theological understanding of that conviction. Given the time and place—1954 in Chicago—the theology was transubstantiation by the power of the priest. For our limited purposes, it is enough to say that at the time that particular theology was intelligible and persuasive for him. It opened him up, made him receptive, to whatever might come his way. Intelligible theology paves the way for religious experience.

This illuminates a crucial principle of religious sensibility—persuade the mind; alert the spirit. If the mind is persuaded by reasonable theology that God is present to all creation, the spirit becomes alert to this presence and can consciously experience it. If the mind is persuaded by reasonable theology that all people need forgiveness, the spirit becomes alert to its own sinfulness and opens itself to grace. If the mind has a working and coherent understanding of Word and sacrament, the spirit becomes alert to their possibilities. The ultimate purpose of persuasive conceptualizations of core beliefs is to sensitize the person to the religious experience which the beliefs reflect. Theology not only flows from the experience, but it returns to it.

The boy-turned-man has lost the theology of his youth. The belief that "Christ is present" remains; but the lack of a reasonable conceptuality for this belief makes him doubt. The theology that was intelligible in 1954 is not persuasive in 1983. When the mind cannot account for its convictions, the convictions lose their power to direct spirit.

Without a persuasive theology, the boy-turned-man will not open himself to Eucharist as he did in the past. His new theology points him in the direction of interpersonal and social situations; and so it can be expected that his religiously significant experiences will be in those areas of life. People mediate the divine; and so it will be in relationship to people that he will await God.

He is comfortable with this perspective; and when he talks faith and theology, this is what he talks. But "deep down inside" he knows his sensitivity to the Divine Presence is indebted to the host that talked without words. He cannot yet make all the connections he senses are there. Like most Catholics today his theology is incomplete and shifting.

He has also made, in a minimal way, the other two mental moves of theology. He tries to appropriate everything he comes in contact with from the perspective of the fullness of reality it lives within. He wants his conviction of "inner radiance" to be the permanent way he sees reality. He is not quite sure how to do this. More creative and constructive thinking is required.

What he needs is someone to help him. And, like most moderns, he is hypercritical of religious experience and its communications. He does not talk about the experience. He is tempted to reduce it to interior psychological processes. He wants to know whether it has diminished or enriched him. Is he living out of an illusion or is he tuned into the depth of reality? Modern critical consciousness has bequeathed an atmosphere of suspicion. This man has inherited it.

The formulation of beliefs and their theological exploration, extension, and criticism is the natural overflow of religious experience. A religious experience that did not find embodiment in myth and ritual would disappear; and a religious experience that did not move toward belief and theology would remain idiosyncratic and unpersuasive.

Once beliefs are established and theologies constructed, they function as legitimations of the experience and guide others to that locale of the sacred.

Imperative and Behavior: Enacting the Experience of Spirit

Jesus told a story, recorded in the chapter eighteen of Matthew, about a servant who was forgiven a huge debt by a king; but who, in turn, refused to forgive a fellow servant the merest fraction of what he himself owed. Although the story does not tell us, we can be assured that the first servant profusely thanked the king for his generosity. There was no lack of gratitude toward the magnanimous master. But when he hears his own recently spoken plea for mercy in another's mouth ("Have patience with me, and I will pay you everything"), he does not recognize it. The forgiven servant jails his fellow servant. When the king hears of this, he calls the forgiven servant before him and speaks these angry words. "You wicked slave! I forgave you all the debt because you pleaded with me. Should you not have mercy on your fellow slave, as I had mercy on you?" Sin, among other things, is having a short memory.

One message that flows from this parable is to "imitate the reality you have known." From our perspective, the core religious experience contains a core imperative. The dynamics of the living relationship to God which comes to mind and heart in the experience of Spirit includes a drive to action. This drive to action is immediate to the experience and might be more basic than the need to express the relationship in myth and ritual and to cognitively claim it in belief and theology.

The ethical impulse is to pass along what has been experienced. The religious grounding of behavior is enshrined in the imperative: "Be perfect, therefore, as your heavenly Father is perfect" (Matthew 5:48). It is also reflected in how people should view the behavior of Christians. "Let your light shine before others, so that they may see your good works and give glory to your Father in heaven" (Matthew 5:16). The experience of God catapults the person into the human world with the divine agenda.

But the core imperative which flows from the religious experience is an overall orientation. "Be merciful, be loving, be just" are broad-based leanings. They are pervasive attitudes which qualify every experience from burping a baby to firing an inept cashier.[11] As basic stances, they direct our energies and ingenuity in a certain direction. But as religious imperatives they do not tell us exactly how to act in any given situation. They provide a dominant direction, but do not immediately entail a specific project.[12] They need to be concretely mediated.

These mediations will always be imperfect translations of the core imperative. The imperative is a transcendent command which can never be completely embodied in any situation. Therefore, there is always the need to rethink and redo, to search for a more faithful mediation. The Christian ethical life is a process of action, evaluation, and new action. This is why many claim that conversion is not only the initial act of Christian identity, but the continual atmosphere of Christian life.

The most familiar instance of how a foundational orientation needs to adapt and readapt itself in order to remain faithful is parenting. The parent's basic stance toward the child is love. For our purposes, we will assume this pervasive attitude is generated not only from the fact that it is the parent's own child, but from a living relationship to God that came to mind and heart with the birth of the child.

At one moment, love plays itself out as protection; at

another moment, discipline; at still another, the setting of boundaries; at yet another, the relaxing of boundaries. The living relationship to God sets the tone of the living relationship with others. The core impulse of the religious experience is diversified into many different actions. An apt analogy is that the core imperative is like a single ray of light which is refracted through the prism of "events and encounters" into a spectrum of responses. Guidelines for parental love can be established, but they must always be adapted to the demands of new situations.

As individuals age, they collect a history of what they consider to be the right thing to do in certain situations. This is the development of personal ethical wisdom and, when consulted, often comes under the heading of "sage advice." With collectivities, the process is similar; but the results are often more enduring, resulting in the establishment of community standards.

A people living in the ongoing conflicts of history develop a tradition of ethical guidelines. In the confrontation between the core imperative and the concrete situation, specific responses are worked out. If this concrete situation is repeatable, these responses over a period of time become either law or custom or just the expectations of the group.

It is important for corporate identity to be able to say not only "This is what we believe" but also "This is how we act." To be part of the creation of an ethical tradition is different than to be the recipient of an ethical tradition. The creators are building the bridges between religious imperatives and concrete situations. The religious experience is alive and well and pushing to be recognized.

Many of the letters of the New Testament reflect this activity of fashioning new responses out of the experience of Spirit. What are the implications of this experience and its core imperative for offering food to idols, participating in prostitution, marrying an in-law, paying taxes, owning slaves, being married to a non-Christian. Forging ethical positions which are owned by a community is a process of conflict, argument, agreement, and disagreement.

Receivers of a tradition are initially in a more passive posture. To be born or to enter into a community of venerable age is to inherit their history of ethical responses. In effect, the communication to the newcomer is "We have seen this situation before. We are Christians who live out of love. The best loving thing to do in this situation is (fill in the blank)."

Often religious and social sanctions reinforce these more-than-suggested behaviors. If the community standards are trespassed, the community's authorities may excommunicate the offender. And since this is a tradition of behaviors based on religious imperatives, the community, depending on how it sees its relationship to God, may declare the offender out of favor with God and predict future, divine punishment. Initially, ethical responses flow from the fullness of religious experience. But they soon become tangled with social systems of reward and punishment.

The enduring problem of receiving a religiously grounded ethical tradition is externalism. The behaviors are encouraged by the social and religious sanctions that have grown up around them. When these sanctions are no longer feared, the behaviors no longer appear desirable. Many commentators see contemporary Christianity suffering this fate. Ecclesiastical excommunication and eternal hell are not the motivators they once were.

There are undoubtedly many contributing factors to the collapse of this particular "sacred canopy." The most cited undermining force is the infamous "secular spirit of the age." But perhaps the more powerful influence is the contemporary religious sensibility. This sensibility tends to make a clear distinction and, at times, a complete separation between Church affiliation and true faith. Not to belong is not automatic disgrace. It may be the only path personal conscience can travel. Also, for many people the love of God has swallowed any thought of punishment. Afterlife, if and when it is considered, is seen as redress for the indignities of this life, not further indignity. But no matter what the reasons, the question arises: "With this external context of ethics collapsing, will the actual behaviors be abandoned?"

There has been a massive rational and pragmatic response to this situation. On one hand, the connection between basic beliefs and various behaviors has been spelled out. The dynamic reads: "If this is who we are and this is what we believe, this is what we must do." This is an attempt to move from external sanctions to internal reasoning.

On the other hand, there has been sustained argumentation that ethical living means good living. If we act toward one another in a certain way, our own lives and the lives of others will be enriched. Sinful behavior may appear to be pleasurable and have personal payoffs; but this is an illusion. The ethical behavior prescribed by the tradition is the path of fulfillment. Ethics is searching for a new grounding in belief and authentic living.

These efforts are certainly in the right direction and have had a tremendous impact on some people. Most importantly, they have brought together two of the major responses to the living relationship to God awakened by the experience of Spirit. The mental activity which flows from the experience seeks, in part, to view all of life from the perspective of the encountered God. The behavioral activity which flows from the experience seeks to act toward all of life as God acts.

These two activities come together in the unity of the person. What we see determines to a large extent what we are capable of doing; and when we do something in a particular way, we see the "object" of our action in a new way. But there is a real question whether Christian action can be promoted by spelling out the logic of belief and behavior. The underlying energy of both is the religious experience. Unless this experience "happened, happens, and will happen," the formulated beliefs and proscribed behaviors will remain groundless.

There is an indication that Christian ethical behavior springs from the activation of the core imperative in the concrete situation. A previous religious experience which grounds the imperative is assumed. Then something in the situation triggers the imperative anew. In the parable of the unmerciful servant, the master "has compassion" on the servant the moment before he forgives the debt. It is this compassion that moves him to a new and unprecedented act. Conversely, even though the fellow servant uses the same pleading words, the forgiven servant "feels" nothing toward him. He does not experience the life of his fellow servant as his own; and so his actions are predictably callous. The hope for new action in an old world comes when the actual concrete situation triggers the core imperative of the religious experience.

This triggering of the core imperative is not a controlled, rational process. Although it deals in the immediacy of insight, it does not deal in the torture of logic and obligation. The actual dynamics of the Christian ethical experience are powerfully revealed in the Lucan account of Jesus' confrontation with the lawyer (Luke 10:25–37). At the center of this confrontation is the parable of the Good Samaritan. This parable could be isolated from its context and its tremendous influence in the history of Christian ethics discussed. But, for our purpose, the contrast between what might possibly impel the lawyer to act and what actually impels the Samaritan to act is important. The distinction is between an argument from belief and a drive from religious experience.

The initial interchange between Jesus and the lawyer is a head trip. The lawyer wants to know what he must do to gain eternal life. In a Christian context, the inquiry is already misplaced. Salvation is the free gift of God, not something to be gained by human effort. The Pauline slogan—we are saved by faith, not by works—refutes the question.

But things are not that simple. The Letter of James is an angry reply: "What good is it, my brothers and sisters, if you say you have faith but do not have works? Can faith save you? If a brother or sister is naked and lacks daily food, and one of you says to them,'Go in peace; keep warm and eat your fill,' and yet you do not supply their bodily needs, what is the good of that?" (James 2:14–16).

The Lucan Jesus will negotiate this tension and bring faith and works together in the dynamics of religious experience and core imperative.

Jesus is typically evasive: "What does the law say?" The lawyer answers his own question with the double commandment to love. And Jesus, the master game player, closes the conversation with a compliment. "You have answered correctly. Do this and you shall live." But the account tells us the lawyer was not satisfied, because he had not yet justified himself. And so another question: "Who is my neighbor?" With this, the trap is set. The one who came to test is about to be tested.

The mind of the lawyer is a maze. "What must I do to be saved?" really means "What am I obliged to do in order to get what is ultimately good for me?" Deducing actions from obligations in light of ultimate punishments is an egocentric labyrinth. A loving response to concrete situations will never survive so torturous a process. The temptation to rationalize rather than truly reason is too great. It is often mentioned that as the lawyer hears the story, he easily excuses his fellow religious elite from helping the man in the ditch. There is the question of ritual impurity and exactly what is the higher value in a situation like this. There are many good reasons for the priest and the Levite to pass by. But the man with the best reason to pass by has yet to arrive.

If we assume the man in the ditch is a Jew, the expected Samaritan response would be, "Good! One less Jew." But the Samaritan does not ask the question, "Am I obliged?" At the sight of the man in the ditch, he is moved with compassion. A new dynamic is happening. He is first of all responding to a reality that is moving him in a compassionate way.

In later theological language, this is the movement of grace. The concrete situation has activated the core imperative that flows from the core experience. But as we have noted, core imperatives are not specific suggestions. It does not tell him what to do. It only drives him in a certain direction. But from what the Samaritan actually does we discover one important quality about the core imperative. It is extravagant. The Samaritan dresses the man's wounds with oil and wine, puts him on his beast, brings him to an inn, pays for his care, and tells the innkeeper he will pick up any further expenses on his way back.

The lawyer answers Jesus' concluding question about who proved neighbor with the resigned remark, "The one who showed mercy." The final, capstone comment is to go and do likewise.

But what is the lawyer to "do"? He is to live out of the religious experience of God's mercy, which will make compassion not the logical motivation for his action but the very reality that carries him into action. In caring for the man in the ditch, he will be responding not only to the man but also to the grace of God as it flows through him. He will not be saving himself but responding to the free gift of divine love by extending love to others.

Faith in God and charity toward others is the single dynamic of Jesus' experience of God. Christian action in concrete situations results from the triggering of the core imperative at the heart of the religious experience. The harsh truth of Jesus' religious vision is that only compassion knows how to act.

Our boy-turned-man has had the core imperative of his religious experience triggered in a number of situations. But, by his own admission, it has usually been activated because he has violated its intention. It seems his actual response to situations has difficulty in moving from belief to behavior. He usually forgets his belief in the fullness of the person and acts expediently.

But sometimes when he has tried to reduce people to their functions and manipulate them for his gains, the imperative has "come back" to remind him of their fullness. At these times, he has managed to reverse his action and find a new way to deal. He is surprised by the continual reemergence of the core imperative. From a developed theological perspective, the most appropriate comment might be that "grace does not give up easily."

But the more noticeable fact is that he has not integrated the imperative into his permanent style of relating. It is only a "sometime" thing; and his awareness of it usually arrives as guilt because he is actively working against it. Consequently, he has not developed the art of treating people in their fullness. The core imperative is not consistently overflowing into the specific situations of his life.

But there is some indication that when he does manage to act in accord with the imperative, he experiences a fullness of life that he cherishes. He touches once again the reality that touched him long ago. In the rarified world of spiritual development, he is at a crucial juncture. He needs to grow more fully and appropriate more thoroughly the experience of Spirit that has been given him. If he does not, he risks losing it.

For Further Reflection

1. Maurice Blondel said, Jesus wrote only once and then it was in the sand. Although Jesus actually wrote twice (John 8:8), the suggestion of that observation is that the depth of Jesus was not a message that could be captured in ink. Jesus' legacy was that he was the bringer of a living relationship with God. What are some of the consequences of this heart-to-heart transmission of this living relationship? How does the legacy of Jesus differ from those prophets who have left a written message?

2. The people of Spirit and Memory have accumulated endless creations that are the result of a ceaseless, dynamic process of relating to both God and the world. These creations constitute the Christian heritage. After twenty centuries of Christian history, the question often asked about this inheritance is "What is essential and what is accidental? What can change and what must remain the same?" What criterion would you use to judge the essentiality of these creations?

3. The following quotation explains how religious traditions die:

   Religions usually degenerate in the end into a rationalistic theology, a formal morality, and a ritualistic cult. When in this way rites and practices are detached from religious experience, they can only survive as a form of restraint which the religious society exercises its members....Sometimes a religion which is nothing more has ceased to live. To take religion in this state of existence and define it as religion is almost the same as taking a decomposing corpse and defining it as life and a living being.

What examples can be brought forward in support of this
description?

Chapter Three

Stories of the Spirit

There can, of course, be no a priori proof of the critical and liberating effect of such stories, which have to be encountered, listened to and told again. But surely there are, in our post-narrative age, storytellers who can demonstrate what stories might be today—not artificial, private constructions, but narratives with a stimulating effect and aiming at social criticism, dangerous stories in other words. Can we perhaps retell the Jesus stories nowadays in this way?[1]

JOHANN BAPTIST METZ

*T*he experience of Spirit is the founding religious experience of Christianity. It is not relegated to the past, but is a present possibility. All the creations of the tradition are reflections of this experience. They flow from it and, when they are functioning properly, return to it. The most immediate expression of this experience is narrative, and that is what our next chapter explores. On the one hand, when we experience our relationship with God, we relate that experience in story form. On the other hand, the Gospels are the narrative renditions of the experience of God Jesus made possible. Our concern is to map the interaction between our personal stories and the story of Jesus as they combine to facilitate and interpret the experience of Spirit. Following is one such personal story.

·❊·

The Nun and the Boy

In the summer of 1961 when I was twenty, I was going to be rich. The source of my wealth was going to be a construction job. The job fell through; and I was forced to do what I had done for five previous summers. Be a camp counselor. Of all the undoubted joys of camp counseling, money is not one of them.

It was late in the season and I applied to be head counselor at a camp connected with a Catholic boarding school. This school only took kids in the fall who had attended the camp during the summer. The reason for this was not disguised. The summer camp was staffed by eight nuns and four counselors. Part of their task was to observe the kids and sort out the saints from the sinners. The theory was that the best way to spot a sociopath is to watch him play baseball.

When I talked to the head sister, she was delighted. Not only did I have five summers of counseling experience, but in the fall I would start studying theology. She said it was the happiest day of her life. Before the summer was over, she was to regret that remark.

The campers arrived on Sunday night. On Monday morning someone was missing his hunting knife. By afternoon a baseball glove was nowhere to be found. By canteen time at nine, one of the campers reported losing five dollars. And you did not have to have "light years" of experience to know we had a thief.

It is difficult to know what makes kids eleven and twelve years old steal. But one thing is for sure. They are really bad at it. So, by Tuesday afternoon, we had the culprit. Since I was the head counselor, I sat down with him.

"Why did you do it?" I asked.

"I didn't do it."

"We found the knife and glove in your locker. Why did you do it?"

"I didn't do it."

"Look," I said, "this is only the second day of camp. We are going to forget this ever happened. No one knows you took the stuff. I am going to return the knife and glove—we are going to forget about the five dollars—and start over. We are going to wipe the slate clean and begin again."

"I didn't do it."

This kid was not afraid of me in the least. And all the time I talked to him, there was absolutely no expression on his face. There was no light in this kid's eyes at all.

On Wednesday afternoon in a rowboat he stuck a fish hook in another kid's leg. And there we were again—me and the kid with no light in his eyes.

"Why did you do it?"

"I didn't do it."

"Other kids saw you do it."

"I didn't do it."

"Stay here," I said. And I went to see the head sister, the one who was so happy to have me.

"Sister," I broke out, "we have a real problem on our hands."

"Before you tell me about it, Mr. Shea [she was very formal], I have a few problems I would like to discuss with you. About the keys?"

"O yes, the keys," I smiled. For you see the head sister kept the keys to the truck and the car on her person at all times.

And if you wanted to go anywhere you had to rind her and beg for the keys. And she would say, "I hope this isn't for beer, Mr. Shea." And then I would have to lie.

Well, on the second day of camp I wanted the keys. The sisters lived in a semi-cloistered area above the refectory which had an old rickety staircase leading up to it. I stood at the bottom of the stairs and yelled up, "Sister, I need the keys."

"I'll be right down, Mr. Shea."

"That's OK, Sister. I'll come up and get them."

"Don't come up here, Mr. Shea."

"I'm coming, Sister."

And then I stood at the bottom of the stairs and pounded my feet, producing the effect of climbing the stairs.

"Mr. Shea, don't you dare come up here."

And then she arrived at the top of the stairs, habit somewhat askew and car keys in her hand. She saw that I had not moved from the bottom step and she glowered.

"You're a very cruel young man, Mr. Shea, a very cruel young man."

I apologized for baiting her with the keys.

"But Sister," I finally got in, "we have a kid who steals stuff and hurts kids. We have to get rid of him. If the other kids don't kill him, I'm going to."

She said that it was impossible to send him home. His parents had dropped him off and then taken off for vacation. They were going to return in two weeks to pick him up. She had the telephone number of an aunt in case of emergency; but she would not feel right in sending the kid home to the aunt.

"So," she concluded, "we'll give him to Sister Ruth Ann."

"Sister Fix-it?" I asked. For this is what the kids called Sister Ruth Ann. She was a retired nun whose only concession to old age and arthritis was a pair of red gym shoes which peeked out from under her habit as she shuffled along. Her father had been a janitor, the rumor mill had it, and she could repair anything; and that was what she did. She went around the camp, painting, planting, and plumbing.

I did not think it was a good idea to give the kid with no light in his eyes to the old nun; but I had just lost twice, so I said OK.

The next morning at seven Sister Fix-it shook me awake. "Which one?"

"Top of the last bunk."

She walked down to the end of the cabin. I could hear her say, "Wake up. Come. I need you."

Then it started. We would be playing baseball; and you would look up, and out past center field would be the old nun and the kid planting something in the earth. We would be swimming; and you would look over and see the old nun and kid painting the side of the chapel. We would be in eating; and you would look out on the pier and there would be the old nun and the kid having lunch—two baloney sandwiches and two sodas. Wherever you saw the old nun, you saw the kid; and wherever you saw the kid, you saw the old nun.

The two weeks passed and the parents returned. They parked their car at the back and were walking up to the refectory where the head sister saw everybody. The head sister suddenly appeared on the porch of the refectory and saw me sitting on the hill watching the parents.

"Mr. Shea, come down here."

"Yes, Sister."

All four of us—two parents, one head sister, and one counselor—sat down together. The parents asked what parents have asked since the dawn of time.

"How is our son doing?"

The head sister launched in.

"You lied to us. You told us this boy was doing all right. He is not doing all right. He has stolen other boys' property and viciously hurt one boy. Your son is very troubled."

The mother began to cry; and the father began to plead. "We know. He has been arrested for stealing, and he has been put back a grade in school. But we thought if we could get him into the academy, he might straighten out."

"Well," said the head sister, "it is Sister Ruth Ann's opinion that we should keep the boy another two weeks."

"But," she went on, "he will not be playing with the other campers. He will be working around the camp with sister. Nevertheless, you will pay as if he was one of the campers."

"Anything," the father sighed.

Now this was a "clean cup" camp. Two weeks of campers were dumped; and another whole new batch brought in. The new ones didn't know the history of the kid with no light in his eyes. They asked me, "Who is the kid who hangs around with the old nun with the gym shoes? Think he wants to play baseball?"

"Ask him."

They asked him. He looked at the old nun. She said, "You go play at baseball; and when you are done, you come back here and we will hoe in the garden."

We would be going out to go horseback riding. The old nun and the kid would be "reconstructing the ark" that was at the entrance of the camp. The kids would yell from the back of the truck, "Wanna go horseback riding?" He would look at the nun. She would say, "You go play at horseback riding; and when you are done, you come back here and we will paint the bench down by the lake."

And so it went for the second two weeks. She let him out and she reeled him in; she let him out and she reeled him in. And at the end of the two weeks, the kid was integrated into the life of the camp.

His parents came for the second time and they parked in the back and made their way toward the refectory. From the hill I watched them. After about a half-hour the parents came out and went back and waited by the side of their car.

I think I saw them at the same time the parents did. The old nun with gym shoes and the kid with no light in his eyes were coming up the path that led down to the lake. Even at twelve he was taller than she was. She had her arm around his waist and a glow on her face like a woman who had found a coin she had long looked for; and with each step she pulled him against her. She was hip-hugging him as they walked toward his waiting parents. And he let her do it.

⁘⧸⧹⁘

In this chapter, we want to further explore an observation hinted at earlier.[2] The silent strivings of the Spirit find a Voice in the Memory of Jesus; and when the Memory of Jesus is heard, the Spirit stirs.

Men and women of today undergo events that, with the eyes of faith, are authorized by the Spirit. But the religious significance of these events often goes unheralded. The Spirit is the permeating energy of the experience, but it is not recognized. The experience is appropriated in purely secular terms, and its God-power does not break into consciousness. We find ourselves in the position of T. S. Eliot's impoverished people, "We had the experience but missed the meaning."

In this situation, the Memory of Jesus is brought forward to uncover the deepest meaning of the experience. Since the story of Jesus is associated with the Sacred, to use it to interpret experience is to disclose the Sacred dimension of that experience. The Spirit is notoriously silent; the Memory of Jesus becomes its voice. The first half of this chapter deals with contemporary experience told in story form and proceeds to the Jesus story. Although storytelling and story listening can never be separated, the concentration will be on personal storytelling.

In the second half of the chapter, we will focus on what happens when we hear the Jesus story. The oldest Christian appreciation of the origin of faith is *"fides ex auditu,"* faith comes from hearing. In hearing the story of the life, death, and resurrection of Jesus of Nazareth something happens. The hearers are shocked, stunned, turned around. Their lives are seen in a new light; and they must choose for or against the God that is breaking into their awareness as they hear the good news.

What is happening is that the Memory of Jesus is triggering a new experience of the Spirit. The story of the Spirit-Giver stirs up the dormant Spirit in the lives of the listeners. The Christian code for this experience is "In remembering Jesus Christ, he becomes present." This procedure begins with the story of Jesus and moves to contemporary experience. In the second half of this chapter, the concentration will be on story listening.

Experiencing the Religiously Significant

Our assumption has been that at birth people are initiated into a living relationship with God. The more immediate relationships of human living—self, family, friends, society, universe— mediate a deeper relationship to the ultimate Mystery of life itself. This relationship to God is alive and functioning even though we are not aware of it. We may be able to blot out the memory of other relationships by banishing them from our minds; but this divine presence is an ontological constant.

Two of the metaphors of Divine Presence from the Hebrew Scriptures are breath and blood. This omnipresent divine influence is as subtle and as influential as inhalation and exhalation of air and the rush of blood. The words on the wall at Delphi are eternally true: "Invoked or not, God is present."

Religiously significant experiences are those times when we become aware of this relationship and sense that some of the effects within us and within our situation have been stimulated by this relationship. Although the practical demands of staying alive are the usual contents of consciousness, there are moments which, though occurring within the everyday confines of human living, take on larger meaning. They have a lasting impact; they cut through to something deeper. It may be the death of a parent, the touch of a friend, falling in love, a betrayal, the recognition of what has really been happening over the last two years, the unexpected arrival of blessing, the sudden advent of curse. But whatever it is, we sense we have undergone something that has touched upon the normally dormant but always present relationship to God.

But the arena of religiously significant experiences is much wider than interaction with the products of past Christian living. In fact, any interaction in life has the potential of becoming religiously significant. Contemporary theology insists that grace is coextensive with creation. Grace is available to us in and through the events of ordinary life. Given this conviction, we sift our personal histories—events that occur in interaction with the products of Church and Tradition and events that occur independent of Church and Tradition—for the touch of God.

Another way to view religiously significant experience is in terms of what triggers them. Church and Tradition have an enshrined set of triggers. Through hearing the story of Jesus, participating in the sacraments, attending Mass, meditating, engaging in certain prayer practices, people enter explicitly into their relationship to God.

But a more extensive set of triggers are found in the multiple-life situations in which people are thrust. In sickness and vitality, for truth and justice, in love and reconciliation, in pondering the vastness of space and of traveling the inner, endless journey of the psyche, people come upon the reality of God. In fact, this seems to be the more traveled path to religious awareness today.[3]

The trigger power of these creations of the Christian tradition is being seriously questioned. The presence that people used to find in the dark back of Gothic churches they now claim they find in the bright light of the secular world. Our interests are in bringing these two sets of triggers together.

But it should be noted that religiously significant experiences of everyday life are not completely tradition-free. There are dual influences. First, the people we are concerned with were socialized into the Christian religious tradition. This socialization may have been more or less successful; but, at a minimum, it opened minds and hearts to the larger realities and questions of life. It initiated a sensitivity to the presence of God in everyday living.

Second, the tradition is often called in to interpret the fullest meaning of what is happening. The creations of the tradition do not trigger the experience, but as the experience is gradually interpreted over time, traditional forms are consulted to disclose the depth of what has happened. The inherited faith acts as an interpretive tool. Memory becomes the voice for the silent strivings of the Spirit.

It is extremely difficult to categorize the different types of religiously significant experiences. The qualities of one type always seem to overflow into the qualities of another type. For our purposes, three interlocking categories are (1) mystery experiences that stress expanded consciousness, (2) conversion experiences that stress change of mind, heart, and behavior, and (3) revelatory experiences that stress the communication of a message. A brief rundown on these types of religiously significant experiences will lead us to our major concern: how people relate these experiences in story form.

Mystery experiences are times when we become aware of the larger Mystery within which we live. Usually our consciousness is narrowed to the immediate issue at hand, whether that is catching the train or getting the sink fixed. Times of mystery move our mind and heart to consider the wider, more encompassing reality of human living.

There are degrees of awareness in mystery experiences. Rodney Stark has delineated four possibilities.[4] Experiences are *confirming* when we simply sense the presence of God. In these moments, our inherited belief has been empirically confirmed. Experiences are mutual when we not only notice God but God notices us. The relational flow goes both ways.

Experiences become *ecstatic* when the two-way relational flow is perceived as loving. That which I notice and notices me, loves me. Experiences become *revelatory* when God lets me in on his plan and solicits my participation. That which loves me has something for me to do. When most people think of religiously significant experiences, they think of some form of mystical awareness.

There may be some form of mystical expanded awareness in conversion experiences, but the major emphasis is on the process of change. The catalytic event of a conversion experience is seldom solicited. Something happens; and the person suddenly perceives her or his life as participating in, what Tillich would call "the structures of destruction." Something happens which throws new light on the person, and what the light shows is not flattering. The person then is free to change or remain in the destructive patterns that have been revealed.

If the person chooses to change, the conversion process is successfully completed. If the person hardens and refuses to change, the conversion process is aborted. The pattern of the experience could be laid out as (1) destructiveness, (2) catalytic occurrence, (3) human freedom, and (4) movement toward new life. If this type of experience is to be religiously significant, God must be perceived as the energy of the entire process.

There may be expanded mystical awareness and change in revelatory experiences, but what they stress is communication.

Revelatory experiences are times when a truth about the ultimate Mystery of life has been received. In these experiences, the person responds, "This is what it is all about." Life may be about many other things; but it is at least about this. Although the experience took place at a certain time and in a certain place, what was revealed is applicable to all times and all places. The truth that was given in the experience is universal.

The truths that are experienced in revelatory experiences are not solutions to puzzles. They are rather felt insights into what it means to be alive. The camp story that opened this chapter would fit most comfortably into the category of revelatory experience. If this type of experience is to be religiously significant, the truth that is received must be perceived as given by God.[5]

These three types of experience become religiously significant for two reasons. First, either immediately within the experience or upon later reflection, a sacred power is discerned to be present and active. These are not just peak times or special moments. They can be investigated from a psychological point of view and the mental and affective processes precisely detailed. They can also be pursued from the sociological perspective, and the cultural influences and social determinations persuasively laid out.

But for the person undergoing the experience what happened cannot be reduced to these two approaches. Psychology and sociology can illuminate what happened, but, in the last analysis, they cannot determine what happened. The experience becomes explicitly religious when it is judged to be a time of contact with a transcendent otherness. Divine reality has made itself felt.

Second, these types of experiences are formative of our religious identity. Every person has multiple identities. We understand ourselves one way in the context of family, another way in the context of work, another way in the context of society, and still another way in the context of Church. One person is a father and husband, a plumber, a taxpayer, and a layman. Another person is a daughter, a counselor at a family life center, a native of Kentucky.

Religious identity includes—yet goes beyond—these immediate forms of self-understanding. It concerns the ultimate self. As ultimate, this identity permeates all our other self-understandings. It colors or, in another metaphor, flavors our familial, work, societal, and ecclesiastical identities. Religious identity focuses on "who we are" in the final analysis and so influences, to some extent, who we will be in all the proximate situations of life. These three types of experience initiate, fund, nuance, or disorientate this ultimate identity. They are the real resourcing and conscious input into the living relationship with God.

Telling Stories of Religiously Significant Experiences

We will use the story of camp which opened this chapter to explore the way religiously significant experiences are told and retold in story form. Although I have opted to use a personal life experience, I hope it does not restrict our reflections to my ego. Each person has religiously significant experiences that are idiosyncratic. They belong to him or her; and they sometimes find very little resonance in other people.

But other experiences are symptomatic of the human condition. They belong to the person, but not to the dimension of the person that is unique but to the dimension of the person which is shared with other people—the affirmations and conflicts of our common humanity. This story is offered with that hope; and, like all true stories, in the hope that it will have an effect similar to the one found in Chaucer's *Canterbury Tales* and trigger the personal stories of the reader.

In general, three components of this storytelling process can be filtered out. First, people tell and retell experiences. Any religiously significant event needs more than one telling. Second, through the retelling of the experience, people form pervasive attitudes and outlooks about the mystery of life. Third, these enduring convictions and attitudes engender a certain sensitivity and precipitate certain moral struggles.

First, we tell and retell our significant experiences in story form. There is more in our experience than we are initially able to appreciate. So we tell the story again and again until we are satisfied that everything in the original experience is captured in our retelling of it. The experience has a density to it that will not be illumined in our first halting and incomplete rendition. The surface of events may be easily remembered and narrated. But if an experience has religious significance, it is because of its inner impact.

It is the inner impact of an event that is gradually sorted out and claimed in the retelling process. We tell and retell it "til we get it right." This repetition makes it very hard on our friends. They sit there and listen, and in their honest moments say, "I've heard it." But the truth is that we have not heard it, or at least not all of it. So we must tell it one more time, hoping to bring to conscious awareness all that happened.

In "the time of its happening" a given experience may have religious potential. But this potential will only be actualized over time through a retelling process. It is important that the telling of the experience be in story form. If we give only the pattern of the experience ("I once found out that people only change because other people pay an ingenuous and creative price."), we cut short the process of personal appropriation of the experience through storytelling. To tell the experience in a concrete narrative ("In the summer of 1961...") is to reenter into the time of its happening. We reexperience in diminished form the feelings and insights of the event. In the reexperiencing, we see it differently and "unpack" its meaning further. Storytelling has a power of involvement and appreciation that the mere noting of patterns or talking about experiences analytically does not have.

Another facet of relating religiously significant experiences in story form is that time is existential rather than chronological. Thus, storytellers create time units in terms of its personal impact with only a nod to the hours, days, weeks, months, and years way of counting. An experience may take place in five minutes or over five years. But however short or long, the time is unified in terms of its significance for the storyteller. The experience I told took place over four weeks. But I talked about it as a single experience. Many other things happened during those weeks which, if I was interested in pinpoint accuracy, I would have to relate. But they had very little to do with the sequence of events that were intriguing me. Chronological time is a mere backdrop for the human process of demarcating periods in terms of their existential power.

During the last few years, I have told that story a number of times, in private conversation and in front of large audiences. Before that, I seldom focused on those years of my life and only barely remembered that set of events. Why I should remember it, ponder it, and retell it suggests an interesting dynamic of personal religious storytelling. We remember past significant experiences when something in our current living resonates with them.

From a heavy providential perspective, it might be stated that we remember what we need. Anyone in midlife, as the teller of that story is, is dealing with the question of what is important and what is not, of where the remaining energies will be spent. This story focuses the question of time and energy for its teller. We tell the stories of the past to ground us in the present.

I have changed the story considerably in telling it. If we

had a videotape of those four weeks, the recording would not sound and look exactly as I have told it. The main characters would all be walking around, and the essential flow of events would be happening, but the very words and exchanges that I have related might not appear.

If the story was told for historical purposes, this would be misrepresentation. But religious storytelling follows a different set of instincts. What counts is the revelation that goes on inside the person. The storyteller changes the surface of events in order to express and communicate this revelation. We are dealing with existential truth and not mere factual accuracy. The truth is built upon the facts and does not play "fast and loose" with them, but it has interpreted them in light of the inner revelation. This penchant of religious storytelling is extremely important for understanding both personal storytelling and the formation of the gospel narratives.

The stories of religiously significant experiences are as diverse as the experiences themselves. Yet, despite the diversity, a pattern of reporting can be discerned. The report is usually an autobiographical or biographical narrative that carries, usually in a covert way, the fullness of what was communicated in the experience. But often an image emerges within the narrative which "kernelizes" the experience. This image does not replace the narrative, but it captures its core. As such, it functions as a code for the experience, anchors it in memory, and is the main linguistic medium through which it is shared with others.

In the story we are exploring, the image is "the old nun in gym shoes and the kid with no light in his eyes." These personal images, garnered from experience, become the secret name for God which each person consults. They are not naming an outside reality, but are construing the relational flow between God and the person.

To live within a religious tradition is to share the images

of that tradition. The Christian tradition urges every generation to experience its living relationship to God through the images of Father, King, Creator, Crucified One, and many more. But as long as the relationship is living, new images will continually emerge. These images seldom function socially. They usually remain the private preserve of the individual. But they are necessary if the continuing personal and individual experiences of God are to be articulated.

A second moment of personal storytelling focuses on the pervasive attitudes and outlooks that emerge from the process of retelling. People are natural narrative beings. They love to tell the stories of the experiences that were important to them. But they also love to share the message they found in the experience.

Few people have the discipline to stay at the "basement level" of interpretation that the story, as story, provides. We move immediately to the first floor, and with very little encouragement are on our way to the penthouse. "This is what I got out of it" flows naturally from "Wait til I tell you what happened." We supply a cognitive interpretation along with the narrative line.

At this stage, the attitudes and outlooks that have been formed in the retelling process are explicitly articulated. Since all religiously significant experiences either explicitly or implicitly concern the presence of a sacred power, the attitudes and outlooks that emerge from the telling often focus on God. A storyteller gives the following explanation.

> As I see it, my minuscule will was linked up with the will that our forefathers called God. I don't know what that power is, nor do I call it God. But by it I live and in my slow, often frustrated effort to learn means of communication with it I grow, inch by inch, into a person more nearly resembling a human being than was

ever imagined by me to be possible. This power beyond my own ego is not altogether beyond it or separate from it. It is as personal and "of me" as the color
of my eyes, is friendly and reliable, resourceful and com-
panionable. But on the far side of "me" it is a mystery
with respect to which I put my hand on my mouth.[6]

There is an aftermath to religiously significant experiences, a
permanent residue in the subject. In this account the person is
formally stating the sensitivity that emerged from her experience. We do not have the actual narrative of the experience.
We have the attitudes and outlooks that developed as a result
of narrating the experience.

The attitudes and outlooks that are garnered from mystery experiences usually concern God. The attitudes and outlooks that flow from conversion and revelatory experience
usually concern insights about people and life that God's presence illumines. The life truth that I have taken from the camp
story is that people change, but only at great cost; and the cost
is usually paid by someone else.

I am sure the old nun had shepherded many troubled kids
before the one with the unlit eyes arrived. And I am sure it
would have been fine with her if he had never arrived. But
arrive he did; and so she took him on. I wanted to exercise
that most venerable of Catholic options and excommunicate
him. She exercised an even older option and was faithful to
him in his sin.

The third component of the storytelling process is just the
natural unraveling of the first two. The experience told in story
form, which creates pervasive outlooks and attitudes, engenders
a particular sensitivity and precipitates certain moral conflicts.
Moral struggle begins with the move from numbness to sensitivity. It is only when we "sense" situations in a certain way that we
construe what must be battled and what must be promoted.

This sensitive response to present situations is at least partially determined by the past situations we have undergone. Who we are is prior to any situation we find ourselves in; and our past history functions as a stethoscope to hear the heart of the present.

Ethical sensitivity has many sources; but when it springs from personal experience, it exhibits a perseverance and power that is unmatched. Walter Gulick, in commenting on archetypical experiences, makes this connection.

> A person's archetypal experiences provide ideals and standards with power to motivate action. A person who has experienced the succor of redemptive love with archetypal intensity has an internalized sense of value which is quite different from the individual who has merely been taught that it is good to forgive and love others. The latter person knows that one ought to forgive and love others, but such a sense of obligation will be quite impotent when opposed by other stronger interests.[7]

Religiously significant experiences often begin in a receptive mode. The person undergoes a series of events. But these experiences eventually influence behavior. People seek to live out the meaning which the experiences revealed.

No one is long in the ministerial game before they know a big piece of it is fidelity to people in the grip of destructive forces. The old nun knew this, never sermonized about it, and never knew she taught it to the counselor who watched on the hill. The teenager dropping out of school has to be pursued; the grieving widow has to be "sat with"; the divorced have to be patiently helped back to trust; the sick have to be visited. What is important is the actual other.

The vast abstractions I so easily fall into are falsification of the real. There are no poor students; there is only Mary who needs some help. There is no problem of divorce; there is only John who is hurting and needs to be put in touch with other people. There is no drug problem; there is only Joan who by noon doesn't see all that good.

For the storyteller the ethical imperative which flows from the experience is "pay attention to what actually is." All that is important is concrete and actual. The abstractions are meant to serve that.

Living Tradition and Storytelling

As we mentioned, throughout this storytelling process the tradition has been active. When a tradition is living, it becomes the eyes and ears of people.

> Tradition is living because it is carried by living minds— minds living in time. These minds meet with problems or acquire resources, in time, which lead them to endow Tradition, or the truth it contains, with the reactions and characteristics of a living thing: adaptation, reaction, growth, and fruitfulness. Tradition is living because it resides in minds that live by it, in a history which comprises activity, problems, doubts, opposition, new contributions, and questions that need answering.[8]

The tradition was obviously at work as I interpreted the events of that long-ago camp season. I suspect that only someone socialized into an understanding of love and sacrifice would read the events in the way I did. There is no escaping the "attention-directing" function of tradition.[9]

But the tradition also works in a more explicit way. It provides a language to interpret the depth of what is occurring. Language is a social phenomenon before it is a personal tool.

People who want to express and communicate a religious experience inevitably reach for the language that is available within the culture. This language has a particular history, and any use of it plays upon that history.

Within a Christian culture to "bring forward" the gospel language is to signal the sacrality of the tale. The story may be about toads, rattlesnakes, and rabbits, but if suddenly the phrase "brood of vipers" appears, a connection is triggered in the mind and heart of the hearer. The introduction of the larger Christian story immediately contextualizes the individual story as a story of salvation.

The Christian experience as witnessed to in the gospel narratives can best be characterized as mythic history. The events recorded took place at a certain time and in a certain place. They are about Jesus of Nazareth and the personal, religious, and political conflicts of the first half of the first century in Palestine. In that sense they are unrepeatable. They belong to the past; they have happened and are over. This is their historical particularity. But they are also revelatory events; they disclose what God is doing in relation to creation. This divine activity is not restricted to any one time or place. It is an activity that is eternally going on. What God made happen in Jesus of Nazareth, God is making happen today. This is the mythic dimension.

When phrases, images, and stories from the life of Jesus are interwoven with contemporary narratives, the presence of God is being pointed to. When, in Ernest Hemingway's *The Old Man and the Sea,* the old man cries out and the author tells us that "there is no translation for this word and perhaps it is just a noise such as man might make, involuntarily, feeling the nail go through his hands and into the wood," we are being invited into a deeper level of participation.[10]

For the simple and unartistic story of camp, the deepest interpretation is provided by the gospel story of the woman who lit a lamp and swept her house until she found the coin she had lost (Luke 15:8–10). That is how the old nun holds the boy, the way a woman holds a coin she has found.

Telling religiously significant personal experiences moves beyond the idiosyncratic when they connect with the commonly shared sacred story. At this moment the personal has "leapt out" of its individuality and is talking about everyone in relationship to God and one another. In terms of the images, God is the old nun and we are the kid with no light in our eyes.

Putting together our story with the story of Jesus is the way we discover the movement of the divine in our lives.[11] To return to a theme of chapter one, the proximate players of human life are what are most obvious. Our stories always include the ingenuity and obtuseness of ourselves and others. When we discern an ultimate author at work beneath the fury of our intentions and actions, we talk about its presence by using the language of the event where this ultimate author was fully revealed.

But, in order to be able to do this, there first has to be contact with the sacred stories. And more than just contact. We will be able and willing to use the inherited stories to talk about present experiences of God only if in hearing those stories the divine has been revealed. Only if we have found God in the Jesus story will we use that story to talk about the God of our own story. In the language of Johann Baptist Metz, which opened this chapter, the Jesus story must become dangerous. It must be told so that life is imperiled and renewed.

Encountering the Jesus Story
As Listeners, Readers, and Viewers

Most people initially encounter the Jesus story in a listening experience. Somewhere along the line someone tells us a piece of the Jesus story. Perhaps it is a mother who reads us a section of the Bible as we sit on her lap. Perhaps it is a catechist who first unravels the tale for us.

Subsequent encounters with the Jesus story often occur in the listening mode. The deacon reads the stories to us Sunday after Sunday. The preacher tells them and comments on them while we sit and try to absorb. A friend has been born again and we are on the receiving side of her rendition of the living Christ. Or we may have the good fortune to hear a professional storyteller fill our ears with the comedy and tragedy of the gospel story. Although we are in the age of the printed word (and many claim that even that is passé) significant contact with the Jesus story still takes place in oral-aural situations.

A second form of encounter is the reading experience. We may pick up the Gospels themselves and come in direct contact with the canonical version of life, death, and resurrection of Jesus of Nazareth. This Gospel rendition may be supplemented by a commentary to help us through writing that initially belong to another time and place. Or we may pick up a life of Christ through its author's insights and find the story making inroads into our consciousness. If we are of an intellectual bent, we might encounter the basic story line in more speculative Christological studies; but, in all these cases, the dynamics of a reading experience, an individual in interaction with printed words, are operative.

A third form of encounter is the dramatic and cinematic experience. This is an extremely popular form of contact today. If people are asked for images of Jesus, they often respond by citing scenes from Pasolini's *The Gospel According to St. Matthew* or Zeffirelli's *Jesus of Nazareth* or the rock opera *Jesus Christ Superstar* or the musical *Godspell* or more recently Mel Gibson's *The Passion of the Christ*. Many people feel this popularity is a misplaced emphasis. But the fact seems to be that these renditions are more fascinating and impacting than the staid socialization efforts of the churches. Also stage and film have peculiar powers of involvement and release which make them apt mediums for the rhythms of the Jesus story.

These are not the only ways of contact with the Jesus story, but they are the major modes. A common element among them that is worth noting reflects a theme we considered in chapter one. It is people, always people, who are handing on the memory of Jesus. We have access to the Jesus story through a chain of mediation, a long line of personal appropriations and retellings.

It is through a parent's instructive voice or the evangelist's artful writing or a Zefirelli's camera that the story is made available. This does not deny the normative nature of the Gospel rendition or the need for a teaching authority to correctly interpret it. It merely underlines the personal nature of community and tradition. The tradition thrives because people reexpress its core stories out of their own flawed experiences and in their own halting voices.

At a time when tradition is caricatured as an abstract burden and community slandered as oppressive conformity, the personal qualities of both needs to be stressed. A story, courtesy of Reuven Gold and Hassidic tradition and drastically reworked by the current teller, is rich in suggestions.

⸙

Held Against the Heart

Once upon a time there was a very pious Jewish couple. They had married with great love and the love never died. Their greatest hope was to have a child so their love could walk the earth with joy.

Yet there were difficulties. And since they were very pious, they prayed and prayed and prayed. With that, along with considerable other efforts, lo and behold the wife conceived. When she conceived, she laughed louder than Sarah laughed when she conceived Isaac. And the child leapt in her womb more joyously than John leapt in the womb of Elizabeth when Mary visited her. And nine months later there came rumbling into the world a delightful little boy.

They named him Mordecai and the sun and moon were his toys. He was rambunctious, zestful, gulping down the days and dreaming through the nights. He grew in age and wisdom and grace until it was time to go to the synagogue and learn the Word of God.

The night before his studies were to begin, his parents sat Mordecai down and told him how important the Word of God was. They stressed that without the Word of God, Mordecai would be an autumn leaf in the winter's wind. He listened wide-eyed.

Yet the next day he never arrived at the synagogue. Instead he found himself in the woods, swimming in the lake and climbing the trees.

When he came home at night, the news had spread throughout the small village. Everyone knew of his shame. His parents were beside themselves. They did not know what to do.

So they called in the behavior modificationists who modified Mordecai's behavior, so there was no behavior of Mordecai that was not modified. Nevertheless, the next day he found himself in the woods, swimming in the lake and climbing the trees.

So they called in the psychoanalysts, who unblocked Mordecai's blockages, so there were no more blocks for Mordecai to be blocked by. Nevertheless, the next day he found himself in the woods, swimming in the lake and climbing the trees.

His parents grieved for their beloved son. There seemed to be no hope.

It was at this time that the great rabbi visited the village.

And the parents said, "Ah! Perhaps the rabbi." So they took Mordecai to the rabbi and told him their tale of woe. The rabbi bellowed, "Leave the boy with me and I will have a talking to him."

Mordecai's parents were terrified. So he would not go to the synagogue but to leave their beloved son with this lion of a man....But they had come this far and so they left him.

Now Mordecai stood in the hallway and the great rabbi stood in his parlor. He beckoned, "Boy, come here." Trembling, Mordecai came forward.

And then the great rabbi picked him up and held him silently against his heart.

His parents came to get him and they took Mordecai home. The next day he went to the synagogue to learn the Word of God. And when he was done, he went to the woods. And the Word of God became one with the word of the woods, which became one with the word of Mordecai. And he swam in the lake. And the Word of God became one with the word of the lake, which became one with the word of Mordecai. And he climbed the trees. And the Word of God became one with the word of the trees, which became one with the word of Mordecai.

And Mordecai himself grew up to become a great man. People came to him who were seized with inner panic and with him they found peace. People came to him who were without anybody and with him they found communion. People came to him with no exits and with him they found a way out.

And he often said, "I first learned the Word of God when the great rabbi held me silently against his heart."

❖❖

Contact with the Jesus story, no matter what form it may take—listening, reading, dramatic, cinematic—is a result of personal mediation. Effective communication within any tradition is always a matter of one generation holding the next to its heart.

How a Story Works on Its Listener

To tell a story, especially one with religious ambitions, is risky business. Sometimes stories fall on deaf ears. People hear and see and walk away. No impact is discernible. At other times, the story penetrates to the center of the receiver and "holds the soul in balance." People hear and see and stay to talk. Something has been touched.

But there are no guarantees. It is difficult to predict what stories will function religiously and what stories will not. The storyteller works in the dark. His hearers bring their beauty and blemish, their resistance and readiness to each tale. Who knows what will happen? Storytelling is always a wager.

Within the Christian tradition the wager is that the stories Jesus told and the stories about Jesus will have religious impact. Two reasons we considered in chapter two make this a good bet. First, the stories of the Gospels are the chiseled result of religious experiences. The gospel narratives are the careful working out of the salvific impact Jesus had on people. As such, the hope is that the retelling of the stories will be recreative of the experiences of which they are expressions. What happened once will happen again. The dynamic sequence is original experience, creative expression, retelling, reexperience.[12] Second, the stories are told within the larger tradition which provide the necessary atmosphere for receiving the stories creatively. Life within the tradition readies the hearer for a meeting with the Holy Spirit when the Memory of the Giver of the Spirit is remembered. The wager is reasonable.

Here is an account of a wager that paid off. The story of the death and resurrection of Jesus is told to a young boy.

The Diamond

When I was a small child, perhaps five or six, my mother told me the story of the passion and death of Jesus. I had heard the story before and I knew Jesus would rise. But for some reason this time the story reduced me to tears. No, elevated me to tears. For the overall effect was that I was elevated. Soaring and crying at the same time. I don't remember how my mother told the story, but the phrase that sticks in my memory is "out of love." Out of love the Son of God died for me. I also remember that at the time it was like a diamond was forming inside me. There was some sparkling, brilliant part of me that Jesus died for. I have had my share of pain in life, but I have never lost that diamond. My ultimate self-worth is something I never question. No, more than that. I call the "diamond" to mind whenever I am distressed. It reassures me.[13]

❧❧

Here is an account of a wager whose payoffs are a little more ambiguous. The story of the death and resurrection of Jesus is told to a young girl.

❧❧

Despair

My first religious experience, or rather the beginning of my religious experience (because I feel it is a religious experience to be alive, so I cannot say "this is a religious experience, that is just an ordinary one") was a very tragic one. I must have been four years old; I was sitting on a little footstool next to my mother, who read to me from a children's Bible about Jesus. I had no contact with my mother, but I loved Jesus, and the more she told me about him, for his kindness, wisdom and patience, for his being a perfect man, grew every Sunday. I was unaware, as his disciples had been, of the signs of coming disaster. I was totally unprepared when suddenly my mother told me about the crucifixion and what led up to it. I fell into an abyss of sheer black desperation. My misery was such as I have never since encountered in my life—which by the way has had its fair share of happiness and despair. If I had at that age known that there existed the possibility of ending one's life, I would have committed suicide. Some days later my mother must have told me about the resurrection, but the blow had been too heavy for me to recover in so short a time. What some people think of as necessary for us to reach an understanding of another life going on around and above and within our everyday life, this was the severest misery to me. I started to distrust the Bible, and what I heard in church. And at a very early age I discovered a difference between the Old Testament Jahweh and the loving father that Jesus taught us. I remember that, although I was very sensitive to my surroundings, I discovered that real happiness exists independently of life's situations, because there is in man an unchangeable, inextinguishable source of happiness, a link with the Universal Life. Although of course my emotions, my knowledge and my capacity for understanding have matured, I have the feeling that my religion of today, my feeling of Unity with all living beings, and above all the certainty of the all-pervading Life and Love from which no one and nothing is excluded, is the logical outcome of a natural growth which began with this first desperate moment of truth when I was four years old.[14]

These two different responses to the story of the death and resurrection of Jesus highlight an essential factor of story listening. The teller should check out with the listener what he or she heard. The question that follows the story is: "What are you thinking? What are you feeling?" Theories of narrative distinguish the implied reader and hearer from the actual reader and hearer. The implied reader and hearer should receive a meaning that the text embodies and the tradition supports. The actual reader and listener may receive multiple meanings, some in continuity with the meaning of the text and the larger convictions of the Christian tradition and some meanings that might be alien to the text and the tradition. In story listening that is formative of faith, an extensive and exploratory conversation must follow the story.

A first sign that the Jesus story is functioning religiously is that it moves the mind and heart of the listener into the religious zone, into the relationship to ultimate Mystery. In order to do this, the story must cut deep, stop the hearers in their tracks, grab the soul. There are often physical signals that this is occurring. Tears well up; attention is total; the eyes close to absorb the impact; the hands hold the head which is suddenly heavy with thought. In the above examples, the story of the passion and death of the Son of God carried both the boy and the girl into a dimension of reality that suffuses yet transcends the everyday world. Both have been brought to a consideration of the ultimate Mystery of human life.

But more is required. The story must fill the "Godspace" it has opened up with feelings and insights that are sensed as salvific. The story not only has the process impact of placing the person in relation to the ultimate Mystery, but it also has the content impact of allowing the person to experience the qualities of that relationship. The man who remembers his boyhood encounter with the story of Jesus talks of a "diamond." The metaphor seems to mean that he is valuable. The Son of

God died out of love for him and that makes him a person of inestimable worth. The woman who remembers her first encounter with the story also has a deep sense of an all-pervasive Love. But there is a quality to it that causes some hesitation. She might be finding this Love independent of life situations. The impact of the death of Jesus may have pushed her away from the conflicts of life into an "escape" love. It is difficult to tell from her account of what happened if this is the case. Further conversation is necessary.

The category of "over time" which figured prominently in our discussion of the retelling of religiously significant experiences is also helpful in understanding the impact of the retelling of sacred stories. There is "story-time" and "chewing-time." Story-time comprises the event of hearing or reading the story. Chewing-time is the subsequent reflection on what was experienced during story-time. Any ministerial effort which attempt to use storytelling must have structures for these companion activities. A religiously powerful story naturally unravels into insights and strategies. And many cherished insights and prized strategies can be traced to the impact of a religiously functioning story. Hearing, reflecting, and acting constitute the fullness of religious response.

Besides the awareness of Mystery and the qualities that "flow from it and into us," a religiously functioning story communicates an imperative. The natural imperative that flows from telling religiously significant experiences is also a component of hearing a story which has religious impact. The religious story has a "must" at its heart. We feel commanded to enact what we have experienced. If we fail to respond to what we have found in interaction with the story, we do so at our peril. Religiously functioning stories communicate a sense of danger. We have been touched at our depths and we must respond from the depths. The man and the woman in our example stories do not tell of the imperative that flowed from the experience. But if they did, we would know more clearly the impact of the story on them.

We need a more action-oriented encounter with the Jesus story to underline the imperative dimension. This story was related at a conference on spirituality and the parables of Jesus.

❧❦

The Landlords

A couple, getting up in years, decided they needed some steady income-producing property to bolster their retirement years. They bought some land that had three houses on it. All were rented; and all the renters had a standard lease. One of the clauses in the lease was that if the renter improved the property, he or she could deduct that amount from the monthly rent. This, of course, was to be worked out with the owner.

One of the renters painted the house and began to deduct the expenses from his monthly payment. But he had not consulted with the owners before doing this. The first decreased check came as a surprise to the retired couple. On their way to church on a Saturday afternoon they stopped by the house to talk to the renter and get things straightened out. They rang the bell. Inside a baby cried and dogs barked. The door opened. They went inside. Five minutes later they were in their car, fuming. There had been a brouhaha. They decided that as soon as this guy's lease was up they would oust him.

At church they head this parable. "A man had a fig tree planted in his vineyard; and he came looking for fruit on it and found none. So he said to the gardener, 'See here! For three years I have come looking for fruit on this fig tree, and still I find none. Cut it down! Why should it be wasting soil?' He replied, 'Sir, let it alone for one more year, until I dig around it and put manure on it. If it bears fruit next year, well and good, but if not, you can cut it down'" (Luke 13:6–9).

Back in the car they decided that they would write the renter a letter explaining to him their difficulties. Then after a while when he did not respond, and they were sure this hothead would not respond, they would refuse to renew the lease. But he wrote a return letter. And they wrote a second letter. Then they got together on *their* property in *his* house. They said, "You shouldn't have done it without consulting with us." He said, "Just because you own this land, that does not mean you can come here unannounced and humiliate me before my wife and children." It always looks different from the other side. They said they did not mean to do that. He said perhaps he should have talked to them first. And the conversation went on.

When the couple told me this story, they ended it with: "Last week we baby-sat for their kids."

❖❖

The story of Jesus is told. But who knows what response will be given? There is a need to determine if the response, both cognitive and behavioral, is appropriate to the story and the Christian way of life. In order to do this, there must be a general understanding of the experience of Spirit. It is this experience that the stories are meant to evoke. But this experience takes many shapes, depending on the concrete situation in which it is heard. What is needed is a normative understanding of the experience. This understanding will not solve the problems of what is a fitting or alien response in any minute detail. But it will set some broad parameters to know when a response has developed in a completely wrong direction. But before we investigate the actual contents of the experience of Spirit, we should look at two ways which the story of Jesus is retold.

Two Ways of Retelling the Jesus Story

We have been considering ourselves as hearers and readers of the Jesus story. But we are also tellers and writers of that story. What we have received, we pass on. We not only inherit a tradition, we contribute to it. What we have learned from the story, we put into the story as we retell it.

The first and indispensable step to retelling a Jesus story is to ask: what redeeming power have I found in the story? There is no escaping this personal foundation for the retelling. Without it, all telling lacks persuasion and passion. We hope that the redeeming power that we found in interaction with the story is not so idiosyncratic that it has no resonance in the lives of others. We retell the story not only to express what we have found, but to communicate and enrich the lives of others. But in order to do this, we must join the chain of flawed and halting storytellers.

Two ways of retelling the Jesus story are prominent. The first is to retell the story in companion language. The story is spoken or written in its more or less scriptural form and the salvific meaning is spliced into the narrative. This way of retelling seems to be available to all people. No special skills are needed. We simply speak back the religious meaning that we have found through the medium of the story in which we found it. This is a typical example.

⁂

Too Much "Busyness"

Jesus visited the house of Martha and Mary. It was a special occasion, as it always was when Jesus visited. Martha was busy about many things, not paying much attention to Jesus but scurrying about doing this and that. She looked into the living room and saw Mary and Jesus in deep conversation. She was envious and said to Jesus, really only to get his attention, "Tell Mary to come and help me." Jesus saw through it. "Martha, you are busy about many things, but Mary and I are sharing our souls." Whenever I tell this story, I always get pushed back into my priorities. The accidentals of my life are always getting out of hand. My "busyness" is always preventing my attending to the people I love; and whenever I become aware of it, instead of changing I get jealous of those who take time for personal sharing and try to convince them they should be like me. It is a strange, perverted reaction and the story always makes me aware of it, and calls me to straighten things out. Life is more than scurrying about.

❖❖

Interaction with the story pushed its teller into the question of life priorities. She came to some wisdom about life and expresses that wisdom by retelling the story which mediated it to her. She necessarily changes the exact scriptural form of the story to communicate her finding. The scriptural form, of course, remains authoritative. Hers is a spinoff. But it is a spinoff that is rich in insights and evocative for other people. She is the latest link in the chain of mediation.

A second way of retelling a Jesus story is to imaginatively recast it.[15] This requires the skills of a storyteller, either written, oral, dramatic, or cinematic. This way does not merely state the salvific impact intertwined with the enshrined narrative. It significantly rewrites or retells the story so that the redeeming power which was discovered shines through. This is the more powerful way of retelling for it hopes not only to communicate what was found, but to involve the listener or reader to such an extent that they experience the power themselves. It is time to wager a retelling of two of Jesus' stories.

All I Want Is What Is Mine

I never saw him. I never heard him. I never touched him. But there were those who did. And they told others, who told others, who told others still, who eventually told me. And now, in my turn, I tell you so that you too can tell others. And so, you see, there will never be an end to it.

Eventually they all came to Jesus. Even at night they sought him out. Perhaps better said, especially at night they sought him out.

He would be seated on the ground before a fire, teaching and telling tales. His disciples would be close around him, a bit officious, warding off the very people Jesus wanted near. They were always saying, "The Master thinks that…"; only to find out that the Master did not think that. Usually, in fact, he thought the opposite. But they never seemed to learn. That is why down to this day we call them disciples.

The influential would often drop by. They would stand, their robes unsoiled, at the outer rim of the fire's light. Their arms would be folded across their chest in grim listening. None could mistake that they were men of seriousness. When they spoke, their right arm would shoot out like a dagger thrust; then return to the sheath of their side. Jesus always said, "Come closer, we can barely see you." They never did.

The adulators would also crowd around the fire. "Hello, Jesus, remember me?" They would sit cross-legged, head in hands, their mouths open, their ears eager for every syllable. They would listen for hours on end, not understanding a word.

Of course, the ill were there. The sick flocking to the physician, as he would say. A man with an arm as gnarled as a washed up branch on a beach. A blind woman feeling for the warmth of a fire she could not see. Sorrowing parents with a crazed son, tied round with ropes, his lips white with froth. The obligatory pallet bearers with paralyzed friend. It was quite a scene. It would be hard to say who, at one time or another, didn't make it.

And, of course, troubles. Always troubles. It was like each person was a secret tale of tears and with him they had a chance to cry. A son who would not obey; a daughter who ran away. A husband who would not come to bed; a wife who would not talk at meals. A tax collector without a heart; a priest without a soul. A land which would not yield wheat; a tree which would not bring forth figs. A lake without fish; a home without heat. Too little bread; too much wine. Troubles—and him there in the middle, the fire leaping, casting a circle of light in the dead darkness of the Galilean night.

Once, while Jesus was speaking, a young man pushed through the outer edge of the crowd and moved toward him. Although there was an urgency to his stride, there was no loss of poise or presence. He was robed in linen and purple. As he passed the fire, the signet ring on his right hand gleamed. He was obviously heir to more than the wind. All eyes followed him, including those of Jesus who had fallen silent the moment the man appeared.

He found a place to the right of Jesus and sat down. Then they found each other's eyes. "Yes?" said Jesus.

"Rabbi," the young man's voice was as imposing as his walk, "make my brother divide the inheritance with me. I want my share of the money."

"You are lucky enough to have an inheritance?" said Jesus. "I myself have nowhere to lay my head." He was playing with him.

The young man did not want to play. "I'm not an heir yet. My brother refuses to comply. All the rabbis since Moses have insisted that if one of the sons wants it, the inheritance must be divided. All I want is what is rightfully mine; what is rightfully mine is all I want. Tell him to give it to me."

Now Jesus did not want to play. "Friend, who made me a

divider between you and your brother?" Then he looked beyond the young man at the gathering of people. "Am I now divider among you all?"

"Rabbi," explained the young man, "the more which I want is coming to me." His voice was as logical as a ledger. "I do not ask for what is not mine. Neither do I ask you to be a divider between me and my brother. I will be the divider. All I ask of you is to command the division."

All who heard him were impressed with the legitimacy of his claim and the clarity of purpose that informed his speech. All except one.

Jesus turned away from this petition and stared into the fire. He did not speak.

Now we Christians mourn because so many of the words of Jesus were lost. The words of the Word of God were carried away with the wind. But, Christians, trade them all, trade them all for the thunder of one of his silences.

When he finally turned back to the young man, the story was already on its way. "Once there was a rich farmer," said Jesus.

"He was well into his middle years. Not like you," Jesus gestured to the almost-heir, "still in the vigor of youth. He was rounded from the good life, as fat as a banquet calf. Not like you, lean and muscular."

One evening, while he was at table with his family and friends, the foreman of his farm suddenly stood at his door. Fearing something was wrong, he went outside to see him. "The wheat has sprouted in a strange way, tripling what we had expected," said the foreman.

"I must see this," said the farmer. He had a servant bring him a torch, and leaving his family and guests without a word, he and the foreman went out into the fields. The blaze of the torch pushed back the darkness enough for the farmer to see the superabundance. Somehow the seed had multiplied. Surplus was everywhere.

"The earth is generous, my Lord," said the foreman. "You are the heir of a miracle."

But the farmer did not hear him. Thinking to himself, having only himself to think to, he thought, "I need bigger barns to hold more wheat."

"Tear down the barns and build bigger barns," commanded the farmer.

"Master," said the foreman timidly, "if we do that, the wheat already stored will be lost."

"Of course," muttered the farmer. "How foolish of me! All this wheat muddled my thinking. For a moment I lost my perspective. Keep the barns we have. What I need is more. Build more barns to house the more which is rightfully mine."

When the farmer returned to his house, his guests and friends were gone. His family had retired without kissing him.

The months that followed found the farmer anxious. Thinking to himself, having only himself to think to, he thought, "How will I keep all this more that is mine from the others who are not me?'

So he hired carpenters to build special locks for the barns. When they came to his land and saw the incredible abundance of wheat, almost white for harvest, they told the farmer, "You are blessed."

"Will the locks be strong enough?" the farmer asked. There was no celebration on the final day of harvest. As soon as the workers had finished, the farmer dismissed them. He wanted to secure the locks himself. When the last wooden bar slid into place, the farmer thinking to himself, having only himself to think to, thought, "Now I will never be hungry again."

Now Jesus stared directly at the young man who was nothing like the farmer. "He never was hungry again. That night he died. Now tell me what will happen to all the more that was rightfully his? Whose inheritance will it be now?"

For the length of time it takes to rub mud on the eyes of the blind; for the length of time it takes to push spittle into the ears of the deaf; for the length of time it takes to breathe life into the mouth of the dead, there was silence.

"Then you won't tell my brother," the young man finally blurted out.

"No!" said Jesus. It was the only way he could say, "Yes!"

The young man stood and began to break through the circle of people, shoving them aside as he went. Jesus' eyes never left his back as he moved farther and farther away from him. Finally, he pushed past the outer edge. He was gone as abruptly as he came. The night swallowed him.

We might want to know more but more is not ours to know. The record is silent. Except that sometimes when Jesus was restless, he would tell his disciples, "Stay here by the shore of the sea. I will go to the mountains." Or he would say, "Stay here in this village. I will walk the desert." When he would return to tell them what the mountains whispered or what secrets the desert could not keep, he would often ask them:

"While I was gone," and his voice would trail off.

"If when I was away was there perhaps any word?" and his eyes would search the sky.

"Did you hear anything?" and he would fumble with words like a man afraid to ask but hoping too much not to ask.

"Is there any news about the young man who, more than anything else, only wanted what was rightfully his?"

Peter hated to see Jesus like this—so tentative and beaten, not cutting his losses like a sensible man and moving on but worrying about what was over. So, as he tried so often to do, Peter consoled Jesus.

"Why bother?" Peter said. "He is gone. You have us."

The disciples were already seated around Jesus. They joined with Peter in telling him to forget the young man. The rich are like that, they assured him. The young man may walk away but they would always be there. There was no need for him to brood. It was natural that some would not understand and reject his offer. He should not expect everyone to be receptive. Did he himself not say that some seed falls by the side of the road and is lost?

Jesus waited till they were finished. Then the Son of the Father spoke.

Once there was a certain man who had two sons. The younger son was a bird. He rode every wind, and played his life out against the sky where all could see him climb and fall. The older son was a rock, centuries could tear at him and he would withstand. He was as secret as soil. He made few mistakes; and those he made, he did not advertise. In his heart the father delighted in them both.

He would often watch them in the field. The younger son, stripped to the waist, would recklessly gather what he could. The row of wheat he harvested looked like the wind had reaped it. A village could eat for a week on what the ground still held. When he reached the end of a row, he would turn and yell, "I'm finished." Then he would run back to where his father was and say, "Look at all this wheat."

"Yes," the father said.

The older son, properly covered, moved over the field meticulously, like a man sensing a treasure was about to be unearthed. He missed nothing; lost nothing. When he finished, he walked silently back to where his father watched. "We still have the crops on the west to bring in," he said.

"Yes," the father said.

The day the father knew would come came. The younger son approached him. "Father, give me my share of the inheritance. All I want is what is rightfully mine." So the father called both his sons together, sat them down at table, and divided his money between them. When he was finished, he asked, "Is this fair?"

They both nodded.

"I have no more," the father said. "All I have is yours."

Within a few days the younger son gathered together his belongings and inheritance and set out for a far country. At his departure the father threw his arms around him and wept. "O Father," the younger son said. He was embarrassed by this display of affection: his arms never left his sides. The older brother, who was watching this farewell, thought to himself, "If I was going, there would not be these tears."

Jesus stood now and walked around the circle of his disciples, touching each of them.

In the far country, Jesus continued, this younger brother was no Joseph. He was without his cloak in many a house, but it was not to walk naked and noble away from the lust of some Putiphar's wife. This younger brother was no Jacob who could mastermind two sheep into a herd. Under the guidance of this heir, the inheritance dwindled and disappeared. And when a famine covered the land, the king did not make him the overseer of the granaries; but a small farmer made him keeper of the pigs. And his fall was so great that he would have eaten the slop they fed the swine, but the farmer would not let him.

In this condition the son who once cried, "See how much wheat we have!" cries, "Who will feed me?" He knows. In his Father's house there is food, but he will have to beg for it. In his mind he writes the word of his disgrace. "Father, I have sinned against heaven and thee. Do not take me back as a son but only as a hired hand." With only these words in his mouth he moves toward home.

Jesus finished the round of his disciples. He had touched them all. He had missed none of them. He sat down again and waited a long time before he continued.

On the hill beside his home the Father waits. He has been there before. He sees his son coming from a distance and lifting his robes above his knees he runs to greet him. The servants who are out in the field watch the old man running past them, his breath short, his eyes never wavering. By the time the younger son sees him, the father is on top of him. He embraces his son and weeps down his neck.

"O Father," said the son, his arms never leaving his side.

"Bring the robe," said the Father. The servants had gathered around.

"I have sinned."

"Bring the ring."

"Against heaven."

"Bring the sandals."

"And against thee."

"Kill the fatted calf."

"Do not take me back."

"Call in the musicians."

"As a son."

"My SON," and these words the father whispered into his ear, "was dead and has come back to life."

"But as a hired hand."

"My SON was lost and is now found."

The party had no choice but to begin.

The older brother was out in the fields. He had worked late as usual. The sweat of the endless day dripped down his face. When he drew near the house, he stopped at the top of the hill. He heard the sounds of rejoicing and dancing. He grabbed one of the servant boys and asked him what was happening. The boy said, "Your younger brother has returned and his father has killed the fatted calf and is rejoicing."

"Go," said the older brother, "and tell my father I will not party with him."

The servant boy entered the house and within moments the father came out of his home. He pulled his robe above his knees and, out of breath but with his eyes unwavering, climbed up the hill to where his older son was standing.

"O my beloved son!" the father said; and embracing him, he wept upon his neck.

"All these years," said the older brother, his arms at his sides. "I have slaved for you."

"O my beloved son!" said the Father. And with the sleeve of his robe he wiped the sweat from his son's forehead.

"And you have never given me a calf so that I might party with my friends. But this son of yours comes groveling home having squandered your inheritance with whores; and for him, for him you kill the fatted calf."

"O my beloved son!" said the father a third time. "You have been with me always and all I have is yours. But if any son of mine was lost, surely this feast will find him. If any brother you know is dead, surely this party will bring him to life." Then the father kissed both of the earth-hardened hands of his oldest son.

Suddenly the father was old. He was a tired man. He turned and moved back down the hill. When he reached the bottom, he noticed his younger son had come out of the house. The robe he had put on him had slid off one shoulder. The ring he had given him had been too large for his starved finger and barely clung to the knuckle. The leather of the new sandals had already cut a ridge on his ankles. The father looked back up at his oldest son. He seemed to be frowning. The sweat was still on him. Between them both stood the father.

The music from the party, that at the moment none of them were at, drifted from the house and hung in the air between the three of them. Suddenly the father was no longer tired. He lifted his robes, and there between the son on the hill and the son outside the house, the joy of his heart overflowed into his feet. In broken rhythm he began to dance, hoping the music he could not resist would find the hearts of the two brothers and bring his sons, his true inheritance, back to him.

Jesus now looked at Peter and said, "Why bother?"

The man who once saw in the flesh of his friend the radi- ance of God saw it again. "Because a man always has two sons," Peter said.

Jesus leapt up. A great cry of joy rang out from him. And from where Peter sat, it seemed his hands touched the sky and his outstretched arms were wide enough to welcome everyone.

These are two of the stories which I must tell you because they have been told to me. And now that you have heard, you must tell others. But if all the forests that ever were cut down; and all the wood from those forests turned to paper; and all the quills that ever were dipped into all the ink that ever was; and those quills put into the hands of all the scribes that ever wrote, even then not all that Jesus Christ did and said while he lived among us in the flesh could be recorded. But I tell you these things, so that we may have life.

❧❧

Images of Love and Power

Two stories of Jesus have been retold. What they will evoke is determined by how they intersect the life of the hearer. And since hearers are always unique people, what happens in the wake of the story is very individualized. Someone fourteen will hear them differently than someone sixty-five. The rich will reflect and act in one way; the poor in another. Diversity of response is the name of the game. But the story of Jesus in the gospels is a witness to the experience of Spirit he made pos- sible. When it is retold, it is supposed to evoke experiences that are in continuity with that original experience. The story of Jesus is not totally open-ended; it is not an inkblot. It has some abid- ing concerns which should be present in every response to it.

The abiding concerns of the experience of Spirit are love and power, which are most fully accessible to humanity through the use of imagery. Jesus' imagery for his experience of God was Abba and King. Abba is the familiar and intimate form of father. Although it plays upon the Hebrew tradition of father imagery for God, it seems to be unique to Jesus. Abba stresses the aspects of trust and intimacy. Most importantly, it is a word spoken in love.

Kingdom of God does not evoke tender feelings. Norman Perrin says that it was a symbol that evoked a myth; and the myth was that God was acting as king on behalf of his people.[16] King conjures up power.

The genius of Jesus was to hold together two images which tend to go off on their own. God is a father who would be king and a king who would be father. The abiding concerns of the experience of Spirit are power and love.

A few remarks about how images function in relationship to religious experience will help us explore this Abba-King experience. First, the images are not the reality. The images illumine the experience, but they do not exhaust it. It is an experience of divine reality which the images seek to serve and so there is always a transcendent dimension that remains un-explored. In other words, the images always break under the weight of what is encountered in the experience. When this is forgotten, the images no longer function as a pathway into the mystery of God and people. Instead they take up residence in the mind and link up with other ideas to form a world-view. Although this in itself is not necessarily a bad move, it is not a substitute for the image as a communicator of a lived relation-ship.

Second, the images are drawn from certain areas of the human condition in order to illumine the experience; but also the experience is allowed to "talk back to" those areas. Abba and King are drawn from the metaphoric fields of family life and government. To call God Abba is to try to experience and understand God from an analogy with the world of parenting. To use this image is to bestow an honor on family living. It is so important a part of the human scene that it can be used to understand the source of human life itself. To call God King is to try to experience and understand divine reality from an analogy with the world of governing. This is also a compliment. It points to the crucial importance of politics for human life. But what begins as a compliment often ends as a critique. For to use the images of Abba and King means to draw the human world of parenting and politics into the experience of God. In this atmosphere, parenting and politics undergoes both affirmation and critique. What is happening in the human world that is congruent with the religious experience is supported. What is happening in the human world that is out of sync with the religious experience is critiqued with the divine command to change. The flow between the world of the image and the world of the experience is two-way.[17] This flow is the key to understanding why Jesus took images from the patriarchal family and the ruling class. In that way, he brought them under the experience of God and urged upon them the necessity to change.

Third, these images are open-ended and, therefore, are in need of further speech to express and convey the true meaning of the experience. In other words, what is the point of the comparison? Is calling God a potter suggest that we are inert matter to be molded as a greater power wills? Is calling God a shepherd designate ourselves as passive sheep? To miss the point of a comparison is to end up in either humorous or disastrous understandings.

> When the psalmist tells us that a united family is like oil dripping down Aaron's beard onto the skirts of his robe, he is not trying to persuade us that the family unity is messy, greasy, or volatile; he is thinking of the all-pervasive fragrance which has so deeply impressed itself on his memory at the anointing of the high priest (Psalm 133:2).[18]

In order to accurately express and convey the religious experience, the image must be further specified by story; and the story
must be held in constant tension with the felt perception of the
experience.

The image of Jesus for his experience of divine reality is
not just Abba, but the Abba unfolded in many mini-stories
and one major parable. It is not just "any old father," but the
father who appears again and again in the conversation of
Jesus and to whom his prayer and the prayer of his followers
is addressed. The image of King is not just any King, but the
King who banquets with the uninvited, gives money to servants, and freely forgives debts. Although Father and King are
images rooted in human experiences that are relatively common, they cannot be interpreted in so general a fashion. It is
the activities of the King and Father who is portrayed in the
Gospels that give the correct content to the image. The words
that this Father and King are made to speak, the attitudes he is
said to have, and the actions that we are told he delights in are
the clues to what the experience is like. We must allow the
abiding concerns of love and power that the images evoke to
be specified by the stories.

In the contemporary climate, the need to relate precisely
the images of Abba and King to the religious experience which
grounds them is particularly acute. For in these images many
people see the distortion of the true nature of Christian faith
and the source of endless oppression. The main charge, among
many, is that they have been used as the ideological bolstering
of sexist and classist privilege. The Father and King God is the
energizing source and validation for the second-class status of
women and the maintenance of oppressive political structures.
It provides a rationalization in the very nature of reality itself
for some of the worst human instincts. To uncover the true
religious dynamics of love and power present in these images
does not answer the pastoral question of their use. It will only

once again establish the insidious tendency of human nature to use what was meant to bind us together—an interlocking of love and power—to tear us apart.

For Further Reflection

1. Explain how the words on the wall at Delphi are eternally true: "Invoked or not, God is present."
2. Retell a personal religiously significant experience. What changes came about as a result of this experience?
3. What obligations are in place as a result of this Dag Hammarskjöld quotation from his book *Markings*: "The price you must pay for your own liberation through another's sacrifice is that you in turn must be willing to liberate in the same way, irrespective of the consequences to yourself." Give some examples of how this statement applies.
4. Ian Ramsey says the following about stories that communicate the presence of God: "The characteristic situation [in which God is known] may be evoked for some by telling casual stories, for others by telling wisdom stories, for others by telling creation stories, for others by telling purpose stories." What stories evoke for you a situation in which God is known?
5. W. Benjamin says that a storyteller's tales are "based on experience, either his own or other people's, which he transforms into the experience of those who listen to his stories." Give an example of a story that has been passed on to you by word of mouth.
6. Recast one of the Gospel stories, either in written form, orally, or in dramatic form.
7. Examine two or more retellings in written form of the life of Christ, for example, books by Fulton J. Sheen, Jim Bishop, or so on. How are the retellings different? How are they the same?

Chapter Four

An Experience of Spirit: Divine Love

In vain, my Christ, in vain, two thousand years have gone by and men crucify You still. When will you be born, my Christ+, and not be crucified any more, but live among us for eternity.[1]

NIKOS KAZANTZAKIS

*J*n this chapter, and in the following one, we will try to trace the dynamics of the experience of Spirit as it is expressed in the Gospel witness. Abba and King have provided the framework for our exploration. The experience may concern many different feelings and insights; but its pervasive atmosphere will be the issues of love and power. Our ambition is a greater appreciation of how divine and human love and power interact. To gain this appreciation, we will inhabit the story of Jesus to see what it discloses to us about God, ourselves, and our neighbor.

A good deal of our reflection in this chapter will be to

explore the foundational conviction of Christian faith: God blurts out his love and unburdens his heart for us. For example, in the story of the baptism of Jesus, the religious imagination paints pictures on the sky to communicate its overriding vision of the meaning and truth of human life.

In this story, the silent sky suddenly spoke love to Jesus in the waters of sin. This seems to be the symbolic essential of the baptism accounts in Matthew, Mark, and Luke. The sky is the primordial symbol of transcendence. In times when faith is strong, the sky is the home of God who watches and cares for all his creatures. In times when faith is weak, it is a wasteland, alternately blue and stormy, which silently oversees the struggles of earth.

In the Gospel story's last black hole at the end of our telescopic eyes has a larynx. The sky speaks. The divine initiates the communication. In matters religious people are receivers before they are actors. In a primary biblical metaphor, before they can be sent, they must first be contacted. The Word of the Lord has to arrive before the prophet can sally forth. The sudden voice from the sky reverses a cherished pose of modernity—the human voice shouting at a silent sky and often accompanied by an angry fist. We fancy ourselves as constant communicators and God, at best, as a good listener. But the story implies a different flow to the divine-human relationship. The transcendent reality begins the conversation, not with pleasantries about the weather but with direct address.

"You are my Son, the Beloved; with you I am well pleased" (Luke 3:22). The word from the sky is Son. Although in this narrative we do not have Jesus' response, we have it elsewhere. As we saw at the end of the last chapter, Jesus speaks back "Abba." This becomes one of his privileged images of God. But it must be remembered that Jesus had the audacity to call God Abba because God first had the graciousness to call Jesus Son. Lest this image of Son go astray, the specifying adjective "beloved" accompanies it. The word from the sky is generative love. The boldness of this communication often escapes us. Not only has the notoriously silent sky become loquacious, but it is saying what we deeply hope for and which we have great difficulty believing. We are loved by the transcendent reality within which we live. The evidence that this basic affirmation is true is exceedingly ambiguous.

Jesus receives divine love in the waters of sin. The baptism of Jesus by John in the Jordan has high historical probability. Scholars think that the early Church would not have constructed a baptism story for theological purposes. In fact the baptism of Jesus was something of a theological embarrassment. In the first place, if John baptizes Jesus, is not John greater than Jesus? Matthew is aware of this problem and in his version has John defer to Jesus. "I need to be baptized by you, and do you come to me?" (Matthew 3:14). But a deeper question comes with Jesus' sinlessness. Why is the sinless Son of God receiving a baptism which signifies the forgiveness of sins? Under the influence of this question, the Gospel of John omits the actual baptism. John the Baptist is the forerunner of Christ and witnesses to him when he arrives; but he does not encounter him in the waters of sin.

However, the accounts of the baptism in Matthew, Mark, and Luke have all the earmarks of mythic history. They are at one and the same time a rendering of the religious experience of Jesus and a revelation of how God works everywhere. The story of Jesus' baptism reflects the stories of all people. In a more precise phrasing, the experience of Jesus, mythically expressed in the baptism narratives, is made available through Jesus to all people.

The interactive center of the baptism story is divine love encountering human sinfulness. That is the symbolic reason why Jesus is in the waters of sin. In order to take away the sins of the world, he first had to take them on. He enters the Jordan not to be cleansed, but to be stained. Unless the Son of God in Paul's language becomes sin, he will not meet us where we are. The sober truth seems to be that the arrival of divine love always finds us, to some degree, loveless. The lovelessness of the life God encounters is not simply a brute fact. We may not have started the destructiveness that characterizes human existence. But at a minimum we have "gone along" and at a maximum we have actively promoted it. We have participated and extended the power of sin. That is why divine love is characterized as forgiveness; and the experience Jesus triggered in people takes the form of repentance and conversion. This dynamic of divine love is accompanied by two sets of tears—tears of remorse for our sin and tears of joy for our acceptance.

But the voice is not the only visitor from the sky. The Spirit descends. As we saw in the first chapter, Spirit is the image for the sustaining and transforming power of God. The Spirit and the voice together reveal the nature of the divine presence which Jesus will mediate. It will be powerful love. The love the voice proclaims is not effete or sentimental, but the ultimate force of the world. When this powerful love is at work overcoming sin, another image comes into play. We say the kingdom of God is present. Kingdom happens when people respond to the power of divine love. Put simply, love is power. But what is this powerful love or loving power doing?

The Spirit descends as a dove. The dove image resonates with the narratives of creation and flood from the Hebrew Scriptures. The Spirit imaged as a bird with outstretched wings hovers over the water at the dawn of the world and the dove returns with the olive branch of peace to Noah's ark. These function as clues to the Spirit's work. Through Jesus, God will be recreating and reconciling people to himself and to one another. The dove of Jesus may contrast with the fire of John. God's advent for John is judgment and separation; for Jesus it is healing and renewal. When divine love meets human sinfulness, the person is reconciled and recreated. Whenever this happens, the ultimate author of the event is the Spirit.

This poetic exploration of the baptism of Jesus has disclosed that divine loving power interacts with human sinfulness in the hope of a re-created person and reconciliation between people. These are the structural dynamics of the experience of Spirit. In the first chapter, we focused on the Christian origins of this experience in the life of Jesus and its continuance in the life of Church, the people of Spirit and Memory. In the second chapter, we construed the creations of the people of Spirit and Memory as flowing from this experience and ultimately trying to lead people back to it. In the third chapter, we explored the story of Jesus as both the interpreter and catalyst of this experience. In this chapter and the next, we hope to trace the dynamics of the experience itself. This chapter will investigate the initiating divine love and the following chapter the responding human love. If the experience of Spirit could be compressed into a single word, it would be love.

In unpacking the experience of Spirit what is claimed, or better what is disclaimed, should be made clear. It is not claimed that what will follow was the experience of Jesus, although something like it may have happened to him. The pitfalls of trying to uncover Jesus' self-understanding are well known; and the impossibility of retrieving his actual consciousness is even better known.[2] Nor is it claimed that this was the experience of the disciples and the early Church, although something similar to this may have happened to them. Our interpretation of the experience of Spirit is not an attempt at historical reconstruction. All that is offered is what the writer has found growing up and living within the Catholic, Christian tradition and interacting in a steady but not preoccupied way with the New Testament witness. It is a rendering of the living relationship to God which is indebted to the people of Spirit and Memory and which, hopefully, they will recognize as their own.

The Human Heart Is
God's Special Concern

Divine love encounters human sinfulness in the heart of the person. Anatomically, the heart is hidden in the cage of the ribs which is further covered by muscle and skin. It cannot be seen; but it pumps blood and is the source of life. When the heart is damaged in any way, the entire person is affected. It is these physical facts that make it an apt metaphor for the relationship to God. The relationship to God is the invisible center of the person. When this relationship is properly ordered, the result is spiritual life. In language used earlier, the heart points to the ultimate relationship with God that is the permeating context of all other relationships.

The heart is God's special concern and the arena of battle. God knows the hidden heart (1 Corinthians 4:5), examines hearts (Romans 8:27), and tests hearts (1 Thessalonians 2:4). He wants more than lip service with hearts far from him (Mark 7:6). He does not trust appearances, but looks at the inner reality of the heart (2 Corinthians 5:12). The circumcision of the flesh is nothing if the heart remains uncircumcised (Romans 2:29; Acts 7:51). It is also the heart which Satan seeks to possess. He enters into the heart of Judas (John 13:17) and fills up the heart of Ananias (Acts 5:3). In one interpretation of the temptation narratives, it is the heart of Jesus that Satan seeks.[3]

God wants the heart because it is the source of action. On the one hand, "the good person out of good treasures of the heart produces good" (Luke 6:45). On the other, "It is from within, from the human heart, that evil intentions come: fornication, theft, murder, adultery, avarice, wickedness, deceit, licentiousness, envy, slander, pride, folly. All these evil things come from within" (Mark 7:21–22). The radical ethical demands of the Matthean Jesus stress interior renewal. "You have heard that it was said to those of ancient times, 'You shall not murder....' But I say to you that if you are angry...you will will be liable to judgment....You have heard that it was said, 'You shall not commit adultery.' But I say to you that everyone who looks at a woman with lust has already committed adultery with her in his heart" (Matthew 5:21–22; 5:27–28). In a similar manner Jesus is concerned about the filth on the inside of the cup which shines on the outside (Matthew 23:24); and the dead men's bones on the inside of tomb that is whitewashed on the outside (Matthew 23:27). Evil and good are not just in behavior, but in the interior heart which promotes good and evil behavior.

Distortions of the Divine-Human Relationship

This emphasis on the unity of the person, interior and exterior, heart and action, is necessary to counteract two serious distortions of the divine-human relationship. The first stresses that the real concern of salvation is the inner healing of the isolated individual's relationship to God. In the past, this impression has led to a privatist form of Christian faith and the anomaly that people proclaim an interior salvation in relationship to God while their external relationships to other people remain destructive. This is not a matter of our inability to adequately embody the love of God which has saved us into the love of neighbor. If that were the case, we would live the Christian life of repentance and struggle, never forgetting the salvation we have received and never ceasing to concretely extend it to others. Rather what occurs is a disjunction, a separation of inner purity and outer action. The intimate bonding of God and neighbor is broken; and it is thought that these two relationships can be pursued independently of one another. Salvation becomes interior and unearthly and is able to be claimed, even though the world of flesh and blood is alienated and broken.

A second distortion that often creeps in when the heart is construed as the target of salvation concerns the distinction between analysis and strategy. What we are engaged in is an analysis, an attempt to point to the core of the question. Our suggestion is that by itself no behavioral modification or systemic revolution will bring salvation. Any behavioral change can be quickly undone once the controls are lessened and any social reform is easily manipulated by those who know how into new and clever forms of injustice. The brutal fact is that no salvific change endures that does not change the heart.

But this analysis does not mean that the strategy is as follows: first change of heart and then behavioral and systemic change; first interior conversion and then new action. Any in-depth appraisal of the human predicament should suggest multiple approaches. Perhaps the more effective strategy is social change, which creates the possibility of a salvific, individual restructuring or behavioral change that gradually leads a person to a change of heart. Although Jesus' ultimate target was the person's relationship to God, his proximate targets were self-serving behaviors and ingrained customs and laws that perpetuated oppression. To use a military metaphor in line with New Testament imagery, to name the battle is not to determine the mode of attack. We are engaged in a religious analysis that should be considered in the Christian struggle for personal and social salvation. We are not proposing step-by-step approaches to the total topic of change.

The Heart As Treasure-Seeker

A Matthean passage about the heart has come under considerable fire. "Do not store up for yourselves on earth, where moth and rust consume and where thieves break in and steal; but store up for yourselves treasures in heaven, which neither moth nor rust consumes and where thieves do not break in and steal. For where your treasure is, there your heart will be also" (Matthew 6:19–21). It has been pointed out that treasure is treasure.[4] The same greedy spirit hoards heaven as hoards earth. What we have in this piece of advice is only a change in the objects of acquisitiveness. There has been no transformation of the human spirit from "take and hold" to "give and receive." It is now spiritual coins that are counted alone in the dead of night.

There is little doubt that this passage has inspired this type of spiritual greed in many frightened Christians. But perhaps this passage is not about investment counseling. Like other imperatives of the Gospels, it is not a concrete demand to act in this way. It is meant as an imaginative shock to reorient the heart.[5] We obviously lay up treasure on earth, not merely in unrealistic attempts to totally secure the future but in realistic attempts to provide for the needs of tomorrow. The initial statement, which suggests we cease this practical planning, offends our common sense. The dangers of moths, rust, and thieves are part of the risk of earth and not serious reasons to quit the survival game. It is only with the final "Remember" that the target of the saying comes into view. The saying concerns the heart and its penchant for false attachments which make it vulnerable. If a house should not be built on sand, a heart should not be left to rust.

The heart, in Augustine's famous phrase, is restless until it rests in God. Its natural love is the divine; and when it seeks love elsewhere, it is destined to suffer rust and plundering. A person may treasure many other people and possessions. But the person as person, the heart of the person, is ontologically oriented toward God. This is the structure of created existence; and although the human person is an open-ended reality in many ways, this is the area that the Bible articulates with the words, "Hear and obey!" It concerns the necessary foundational orientation for creative living. When the heart of the person treasures God, all the other treasures are treasured correctly. The deep question of the heart can be phrased "either-or, either heaven or earth. But the more inclusive understanding is "both-and," both heaven and earth. The heart authentically set on God is appreciative of all creation.

The Human Heart Desires Divine Love

Theories of revelation often begin by constructing the human condition so that it is open to God. In the metaphoric language we have been using, they examine the heart. This openness to God is characterized as the capacity to receive, but not to grasp. It is an ascending movement which, by itself, can never attain that toward which it ascends. But God, in an outpouring of love, descends to meet the ascending human spirit. This is the experience of revelation, a human reaching that cannot reach is met by free, divine descent. To keep divine initiative always in the forefront of revelation, it is often stated that the very reaching of the human person is inspired by the grace of creation. The grace of creation provides the possibility of the grace of revelation.

But what is often lacking in these theories, as in most metaphysical renderings of the God-humankind relationship, is the note of passion and panic. Waiting for God to descend is, for most people, not a time of quiet patience. It is a time of furious search and the banner phrase "You would not be searching for me if I had not already found you" is not as consoling as it is meant to be. The heart thrashes about, frantic that what it was made for either is not or does not want it. When Burt Lahr, who played Estragon in *Waiting for Godot*, was asked to sum up his part, he replied, "Hunger!" The heart is a hunger and a thirst; and it needs the food and drink of God. But if this food and drink is not forthcoming, it will find substitute nourishment. To uncover the heart is to uncover desire; and the desire does not merely burn, it rages.

A good guide to the heart as a structure of desire is

Sebastian Moore.[6] He asks the question: "Is there some state of being which everybody wants?"[7] He answers that we all desire to be desired by the one we desire. If we do not desire someone, we are not unduly disturbed if we are not desired by that person. But if we desire someone, we desperately want to be desired back. When we kiss, we want to be kissed back. Charlie Brown has put it both poignantly and flippantly: "Nothing spoils the taste of a peanut butter sandwich like unrequited love." No one escapes this structure of desire. It is universal to the human condition.

But is there also a common object of desiring? Moore suggests that there is. We all want to know we are significant for the unknown reality that is our origin and our destiny. "If our human self-absorption is at root our dialogue with our unknown origin, it is not the self-absorption of the lover awaiting the news that the other is interested."[8] This is the "preconscious" love affair with God. At first we may not be aware of this desire. What seems more immediate and real is our desire for human love. But upon reflection we may perceive that "our questioning of the human beloved is perhaps powered by and modeled on that questioning of God which is the very heart of a person's life."[9] But does the ultimate Mystery of life, out of which we came, in which we subsist, and back to which we will go, desire us? No one of us asked to enter this Mystery and few of us will ask to leave it. But enter we did and exit we will. Now does this strange reality, this other-than-we are which is intimately involved with us, cherish us in our coming and staying and going? For we surely cherish this Mystery.

The evidence is ambiguous. At one moment time, which is at the core of the Mystery of life, seems to be a friend, holding out the possibilities of fulfillment. At another moment, time appears as an enemy, contributing only to our diminishment. Add to this the steady bounty of nature and its sudden fickleness, providential deliverance from danger and freakish chance destruction, the history of human goodness and the chronicle of moral evil—and the enigma deepens. The reality that sums up this ambiguity is death. Our best smile at the graciousness of life is met by the smirk of death. We are inescapably bound to the processes of diminishment; but we are not reconciled to this destiny. Is our desire to be desired by the Mystery within which we live ultimately thwarted?

Two Strategies of the Waiting Heart

This ambiguity—that life is given but not guaranteed and therefore perhaps not returning our love—is the abiding sensitivity of religious awareness. In the midst of this ambiguity what we often do is choose certain events as revelatory of an answer to the question of desire. If we choose gracious events, our sense is that we are desired and we integrate all the horror of life into this fundamental sense of our desirability. We struggle with the problem of evil. If we choose destructive events, our sense is that we are indifferently considered if we are considered at all. In this posture, we reduce all the graciousness of life to momentarily but not lasting reprieves from its true hostility toward us. We struggle with the problem of good. The options often become nihilism or faith.[10]

But our exploration will take us into different territory. We will not look immediately at the various events people choose as revelatory of an answer to the question of the heart's desire. We wanted to trace the strategies that the heart employs in the face of a non-answer. The heart, with its desire skyward but the sky silent, is panicky, unsure, shaken. This panic may induce momentary paralysis. But soon, consciously or unconsciously, protective plans are devised.

F. Scott Fitzgerald is cited as saying: "The three worst things in life arc to lie in bed and not to sleep; to wait for one who does not come; to try and please and not be able." The atmosphere of the heart we are considering lies in bed, but it does not sleep; it is the heart that cannot find rest. But its sleeplessness is not inactivity. Rather in its sleeplessness it takes two different but complementary tacks. The first is to court the attitude of waiting for one who does not come and live in rejection. The second is to try and please and not be able and to live in envy.

The front the rejected heart puts up is that "I don't care whether you come for me or not. In fact, I am not worthy of your love, am I? And to prove it I will kill or whore or rob. Or I will wallow in all the diminishments that surround and suffuse life; a lacking person loves life where it is lacking." But the deep center of the heart that waits for one who does not come hungers and thirsts and cries out:

"Come to me!"

The front the envious heart puts up is that "there is none like me. I have done well where others have not. Other people look at me with envy. They acknowledge my accomplishments and know that I am someone to be reckoned with. This is not just anyone you are dealing with, but a person of distinction." But the deep center of the heart that tries to please and is not able cries out: "None of these things is me. Find me and love me!"

The energy of both the rejected and envious hearts is its raging desire to be desired by that which it desires. If this desire could be met, all the destruction that this unmet desire unleashes might be redirected. The question would no longer be: "How does an empty heart deal with its emptiness?" The question would be: "How does a full heart overflow?" Jesus initiated the experience of Spirit by filling the heart, by revealing that the divine desire for the human not only matched but exceeded the human desire for the divine. He bared the human heart in its fear and panic and exposed the divine heart in its overwhelming love.

The Rejected Heart

The heart that waits for one who does not come lives in the secret yearning for love to arrive. But it has waited for so long that it begins to revile itself for waiting. It seems to stand watch through a night that has no dawn. Like all realities that wait and watch, the heart talks to itself. "Fool, you are spurned! Settle for it." But no matter how much common sense tells the heart to stop hoping, it will not stop. The very fact the yearning will not go away makes the heart feel a dupe of its own desires. It begins to rage and strike back at the Mystery it loves but which will not love it in return. It proclaims itself the Rejected One and plays out this rejection in all it does. But deep down, unquenchable, it cries out, "Come to me!"

The Gospel of John, remembering Isaiah, suggests that the heart and eyes are closely connected. "He has blinded their eyes / and hardened their heart, / so that they might not look with their eyes / and understand with their heart and turn— / and I would heal them" (John 12:40). And Matthew has an instructive passage on the spiritual significance of eyes. "The eye is the lamp of the body. So, if your heart is healthy, your whole body will be full of light; but if your eye is unhealthy, your whole body will be full of darkness. If then the light in you is darkness, how great is the darkness!" (Matthew 6:22–23). The foundational orientation of our heart becomes the way we perceive the events of life. We do not see "neutrally." We select and choose on the basis of disposition and attitude. The old jingle, "Two men looked out from prison bars! One saw mud, the other stars" reflects this fact. The heart sees and what it sees reveals both its pain and joy.

What does the rejected heart see? It sees everything in its devalued form; it reduces everything to the lowest common denominator. Nothing true, good, or beautiful flourishes in its sight. In sexual love it perceives lust; in sacrifice and dedication, guilt; in charity, condescension; in political skills, manipulation; in the powers of the minds, rationalization; in peacefulness, ennui; in neighborliness, self-interest; in friendship, opportunism. The vitality of the old is pathetic; the exuberance of the young is immature; the steadiness of the middle aged is boredom. The rejected heart lives in resentment and demeans all it surveys. And when in the course of events, as often happens, sex falls to lust, sacrifice is grounded in guilt, charity reveals condescension, political skills manipulate, the mind vacillates, peace sleeps, and neighborliness and friendship turn ego-centered, the rejected heart gloats. It does not grieve that life has been devalued; it dances that it has been proven right. All of these realities are as empty as the heart itself.

As we see, so we act. The spurned heart strenuously acts out its rejection in destructive behavior. Since its self-worth is lacking, everything is permitted. It approaches the situations of life out of an inner hostility and so creates hostility in every interaction. It is not coerced by the sanctions of society or moved by appeals to human dignity. Human dignity is a category for people whose eyes have not been opened to their fundamental rejection; and the right ordering of society is merely the protective covering the weak need for meaning. Any behavior is acceptable; and the most unacceptable behavior is the best. Each act that tears down and destroys symbolizes the unloved center which the rejected heart takes as its premier truth. In the Gospels, the rejected heart energizes the behavior of Mary who is a whore, Zacchaeus who is a thief, Matthew who milks his people, the adulterous woman, and the whole class of people known as "tax collectors and sinners." But no matter how hardened this heart appears, there is still in it a hunger and thirst for one who does not come.

But there is also a more passive acting out of the rejected heart. This way does not strike back at the Mystery of life it desires. It accepts its rejection by being nobody. It seeks out situations where life is lacking, for it loves the lack of life. This strategy of rejection attempts to crush all desire. The spurned heart compounds the ignominy of poverty by deigning it appropriate for one so unlovable. It willingly makes itself the footstool for the feet of those more worthy. It bows its head in obedience, not because it hears the author of life, but because a nonassertive self is the natural meekness of a heart that is not cherished. It makes a home in the places where life is perishing. It embraces diminishment, but does not understand the paradoxes of which Paul sings:

> We are treated as imposters, and yet are true; as unknown, and yet are well known; as dying, and see—we are alive; as punished, and yet not killed; as sorrowful, yet always rejoicing; as poor, yet making many rich; as having nothing, and yet possessing everything (2 Corinthians 6:8–10).

The rejected heart that resigns itself to rejection lays down and dies long before breath is gone.

In the Gospels, the heart resigned to rejection is symbolized by the poor, the sick, the forgotten, the insignificant, the outcast. Those who are sure they are not loved; and lead lives of quiet lovelessness. But their surface resignation is not the whole story. The longing to be significant in the eyes of the beloved is never totally dead. This diminished acting out of rejection suffers the same inner agitation as the strenuous acting out of rejection. This heart may appear to have lost its appetite for life; but there is still in it, deep down, a desire for the one who does not come. The ear is cocked for his footstep; the eyes dart about for his face.

The Envious Heart

There is a second complex response of the heart that cannot sleep. Unlike the heart who waits for one who does not come, this heart does not strike back at the rejection or resign itself to lovelessness. This heart begins a process of beautification. It says to itself, "Perhaps at the moment there may be some doubt about God's love for me. But I am going to make myself loveable. When I am done I will be so desirable that God will not be able to resist loving me." This heart launches a campaign to prove its desirability. The lack at the center of this heart is quickly filled with attention-attracting schemes. This is the heart that tries to please and is not able.

The means that this heart chooses to make itself desirable is, quite simply, whatever is available. It may be a radiant smile, an "A" on a report card, new clothes, a promotion. The classic "objects" we seek and then use to establish our self-worth are wealth, power, sex, and fame. All these things are good in themselves. It is the service they are put to that is questionable. The panicky heart uses them to entice love from a reluctant God. Their message is "How can you not love me when I am so personable, bright, well dressed, rich, powerful, sexy, well known?" This heart takes whatever it has and whatever it can get and parades it before the sky—which remains silent.

It is trying to please, but it is not able. Once our waiting hearts begin this process of preening and strutting, we are on our way to a life of anxious striving, self-deception, and oppression. If it is wealth that will make us lovable, we notice we never have enough. A Rolls-Royce tools by our Cadillac on the expressway and suddenly we feel poor. That certain amount of wealth and possessions that we thought would satisfy us never does. We need more; but, as we acquire it, even more looms before us. Our infinite appetite devours every finite appeasement. There is always somebody with more; and whenever we are with them or hear of them, we feel less desirable. Feeling less desirable, we redouble our efforts at gaining the possessions that promise us "self-worth at the center." But when this new acquisition is proudly in our hands, it does not quiet the question in our heart. So we look around, and begin again. We live a life of anxious and hopeless striving.

This dynamic of making ourselves desirable is closely associated with idolatry. Idolatry is often stated as making a finite reality the object of ultimate concern. The finite reality takes up residence in the "God-space" that is the heart of the human person. It promises what God promises but fails to make good on those promises. In our analysis, God remains God and the "object" of the heart's ultimate concern. The question is how to attract divine attention and love. The display of talent and possessions is the strategy employed. But when we do this, we unconsciously equate our self-worth with that part of us we put on display. The totality of the person is tied to one segment of the person. The mystery of who we are in relation to all there is, is restricted to the "stuff we strut." It is the classic situation of getting more and more of less and less. That is why when the heart is liberated from this confining process, it experiences life as enlarged; and the image most often used is "freedom from bondage."

The anxious striving is never over and life becomes narrowed to what we strive for. But that is only the beginning of the bondage of the heart that tries to please and is not able. The next stage is self-deception. Wealth is the perennial whipping boy of religion; but the Gospels are equally interested in the way we use "goodness." When being good makes us lovable and constitutes our self-worth, we dare not do wrong. Wrong threatens the very essence of who we are. Yet, inevitably we do wrong. Sin runs deep in us and breaks out in ways we do not expect. The generous deed is done for self-serving motives. We are silent in the face of unjust systems we are benefiting from. There are no innocents east of Eden.

Yet the heart that has prided itself on purity cannot admit to any wrongdoing. It would threaten the very foundations of its lovability. So we protect ourselves by denying the wrong we do. We hide from the light and rationalize away the evil we are involved in. Since we have identified ourselves so thoroughly with our goodness, we cannot stand the void we would face if it were stripped away. Rather than the terrible truth we settle for the comfortable lie.

Anxious striving and self-deception move outward in oppression. This heart only knows who it is when it knows who it is not. If it is our knowledge that makes us lovable, then we have a vested interest in other people's ignorance. If it is our wealth, we have a personal stake in other people's poverty. If it is our goodness, then other people must be designated sinners. If it is prestige, then other people must be downtrodden. We only know ourselves as lovable when other people do not have the possessions or qualities that makes us lovable. Making ourselves lovable means making other people unlovable. All our efforts to build ourselves up mean that other people are automatically put down. At one level of our consciousness, this life of chronic comparison is too distasteful to admit. But at a deeper, and usually suppressed, level it flourishes. We are now at the insidious center of this heart, the energy source of its strivings, deceit, and oppression. We live in envy.

The heart that tries to please and is not able sees everyone else as more or less pleasing. The more pleasing are "beating out" this heart for the minimal amount of love that the Mystery of life is willing to give. And so it schemes to take their pleasing qualities or possessions away from them. We torch a reputation for goodness to secure our own self-righteousness. We climb the economic ladder, delighting in the fact we leave people behind on lower rungs. Those perceived as more pleasing we

struggle to surpass or demean; those perceived as less pleasing
we keep in their place. This heart is ingenious at actions that
are continual reminders of its own superiority. We flaunt our
higher position so other people do not forget their lower status. We preen our beauty to remind the ugly of their mirror.
We parade our learning so the empty-headed will not presume
to question us. Ego maintenance and defense is now our full-
time activity. And we stand before the silent sky and pray the
only prayer we can: "God, I thank you that I am not like other
people: thieves, rogues, adulterers, or even like this tax collector" (Luke 18:11). In the Gospels, the envious heart energizes
the wealthy, the political authorities, and the religious elite. In
particular, the Pharisee symbolizes the envious heart.

Jesus Brings Divine Love to Distorted Human Hearts

He "needed no one to testify about anyone; for he himself knew
what was in everyone" (John 2:25). Mainly Jesus was aware
of what was not in the human heart. Divine love was missing.
If it arrived, a new way of seeing and behaving was possible.
But God seldom makes independent interventions. The way
divine love would embrace these twin distorted hearts was
through the human love of Jesus. James Mackey spells out the
logic of this divine-human conspiracy.

> In the end the only way to give people the experience
> of all life and existence as enabling and inspiring grace,
> the only way to give them the experience of being them-
> selves grace and treasure, is to treat them as treasure
> and to be gracious to them. Human kind as a class, of
> all species of object on this earth, is very class con-
> scious. The sun may indeed rise on the evil and the
> good, and the same rain refresh the just and the unjust

(Matthew 5:45), but the lesson will likely enough be
lost on me unless the warmth of another human being
envelop me, unless some other human person refresh
the weariness of my defeated days. I simply will not
feel my own life, my own self, as grace or gift of God,
unless someone values me. That is presumably why the
gospels can make Jesus describe the whole experience
of the reign of God, which it was his whole mission in
life to give us, in terms of serving the needs of others. It
may seem, at first blush, to stand the whole logic of the
experience of the reign of God on its head, putting the
effect before the cause. The logic should surely read:
first feel all life and existence as gift or grace, then feeling the grace of God, be gracious to others. Not, first
feel the grace of some human presence, feel forgiven,
accepted, served, then begin to feel all life and existence a grace, and then feel inspired to be gracious to
others. But it is really a universal human idiosyncrasy
that is operative here, not a matter of logic. It may well
be that some rare individual, perhaps Jesus himself,
followed the former logic, having a power of perception and evaluation and acceptance far beyond the ordinary. Indeed in the case of Jesus, it is very likely that
his power to value went far beyond anyone's ability to
value him. But for the rest of us, we can only sense
ourselves and our world valued and cherished by God
when we feel valued and cherished by others.[11]

Divine love is perceived through the struggles of human love.
The arms of God embrace us through the human arms that
hold us.

In those rare moments when we are in the grip of logic it is
undeniable that, as John says it, "God first loved us." But we
come to this conviction by a circuitous route. It is in and

through people's love for us that we sense a greater love. We intuit that their love is not merely of their own making, but that they are symbols of "something greater." Once we have this awareness, we can select out the "something greater" and claim that the unconditional care of this reality is the necessary grounding and motivation for our love for one another. But first we had to have had the appreciation of the divine and this, for most of us, is the gift of loving, transparent persons.

Mackey intimates that Jesus might have been an exception to this process. Historically reliable material has always been lacking in this area; but Christian piety has been quick to fill in the gaps. Jesus found love from the woman who treasured him in her heart. He was the beloved son of Mary who experienced himself as the beloved Son of God. It is also speculated that Joseph taught Jesus the path of love. If Jesus was to use the image of father for his relationship of love and election with God, his relationship with his earthly father must have been life-giving. John the Baptist also enters the picture. Although their messages are quite different, all the gospels stress the connection between Jesus and John. When Jesus hears of John's death, he "withdrew from there in a boat to a deserted place by himself" (Matthew 14:13). This may have been to size up the new political situation; but it also may have been to grieve for a friend. If Jesus was truly human, the social fabric of human mediation must have been an influence, but perhaps not the sole influence, in his awareness of divine love.

But if the Gospels are relatively silent about who mediated God's love to Jesus, they are eloquent about Jesus mediating God's love to other people. This mediation did not occur independent of or alongside of Jesus' human love. The divine worked in and through the human in Jesus. Jesus loved people with such intensity and perspicacity that he drove the ambiguity out of their heart. Their relationship with him became the event which they took as disclosive of ultimate truth and meaning.

Under the impact of his love, people replied, "Yes! This is the reality I desire desiring me!" Part of this response was generated by the fact that Jesus loved people in the very "place" they could not love themselves—their hearts. He did not do this by denying their sin, by accepting them in a gush of romantic blindness. He became the revelation of God by unflinchingly incorporating all the non-love into the power of the ultimate Love he radiated. Any event which qualifies as a revelation of God does not pick and choose in order to appear inclusive. It gathers in everything and through this universal embrace transforms it. Such was the love of Jesus as it sought out the rejected and envious hearts.

The Impact of Jesus' Love

This human mediation of divine love is the beginning of a response to what Sebastian Moore suggests is the lurking fear of all religion. We fabricated the story of God's love. Our need was so great and our pain so unbearable that we fantasized a divine lover to hold us. We are caught in wish fulfillment, daydreaming love without the backing of reality. We need the courage to face the indifference of the universe; and, as Freud so provocatively put it, leave heaven to the sparrows. A major way to put this fear to rest is to point to an event of human loving that broke the bounds of the humans involved, an event that was not individual heroism against the grain of a graceless Mystery, but a revelation of the true rhythms within which "we live and move and have our being" (Acts 17:28). Such was the event of love that Jesus made possible.

Human love that is revelatory of the divine is nothing if not concrete. It meets the need of the other person as an actual other, not as a projection of itself. It attends to the other person on the terms that will open that person to divine love. It discerns the escalating value of every encounter and promotes it. The art of loving is adaptation to the redemptive power of God already at work in the other person. It necessarily employs diverse strategies. These are not coldly calculated plans or unfeeling ploys. They begin with passionate resonance to what is actually happening in the person and evolve into creative responses. Love in the concrete is an act of imagination which knows when to hold a sobbing body and when to let it sob.

Jesus loved concretely. He approached the rejected and envious hearts in different ways. To the rejected, he became an event of inclusion; to the envious, he became an event of unmasking. To the bereft, he became a banquet; to the self-righteous, a mirror. His acceptance of sinners with their rejected hearts and his anger at the Pharisees with their envious heart were two stratagems of a single love. He did not love one group and hate the other. He loved them both in ways he hoped would open their hearts to the love of God. It is easy to see love in the acceptance of the rejected heart of the outcast; but it is difficult to see it in his rage at the envious heart of the religiously righteous. But in the twenty-third chapter of Matthew after Jesus' anger is spent and the litany of woes over, the force behind his tirade is revealed. "Jerusalem, Jerusalem...how often have I desired to gather your children together as a hen gathers her brood under her wings, but you were not willing!" (Matthew 23:37). The vulnerable love of the Son of God is showing.

The ultimate aim of the human love that mediates the divine is to heal the heart in relationship to God and bring the people together. The ambition of divine love is human peace. Some contemporary scholars have surmised that the guiding purpose of Jesus' ministry was the restoration of Israel.[12] He wanted the divided house of Israel to be whole. This meant reconciling the multiple warring factions. The broad categories of the gospels divide them into the religiously outcast and the religiously righteous.[13] They are actual historical people, but they also symbolize permanent temptations of the human spirit. The religiously outcast embody the rejected heart; the religiously righteous embody the envious heart. Although both suffer from the same malady, they are not friends. The ways that they have responded to their inner panic of unworthiness keep them apart. But their surface antagonism for one another hides a deeper mutuality.

The social interaction of these two hearts provide subtle reinforcement for their peculiar distortions. They live with one another in a sick symbiosis. The envious heart delights that there are people who are less than it. Social outcasts and diminished people are sources of the continual reassurance it needs. It whispers this comfort to itself. "There but for the grace of God go I. I am not like them, therefore I am somebody. They are reprehensible, therefore I am approved." This unveiled contempt is just what the rejected heart finds supportive. What it knows about itself—that it is not worthy of love—is confirmed by the envious heart's disdain. And the more the rejected heart acts out its foundational sense of unworthiness, the more the envious heart is justified in inflating its virtue. The sinner and the Pharisee help each other maintain their separate distortions. This is what Jesus saw so clearly.

Reconciliation

Jesus' twin strategies of love are aimed at the distinct distortions of each heart; and are meant to bring them together in common recognition of their sinful grounding and common gratitude for God's healing. The story of the woman taken in adultery shows the "lightening fast" process at work. The sinful woman is brought to Jesus. "In the law, Moses ordered such women to be stoned. What do you have to say about the case?" Envious hearts have found a rejected heart to reassure their virtue. Jesus holds up the mirror of love to the envious. "Let the man among you who has no sin be the first to cast a stone at her." As Jesus scribbled on the ground, they sulked away. When he looks up, his first words are, "Woman, where did they all disappear to?" Then Jesus comments that since they have not condemned her, neither will he. To the rejected heart the strategy of love is acceptance. She is to go, but sin no more. In Augustine's magnificent comment, "Only two are left: misery and mercy."

But the divine love that flows through the human love of Jesus wants everybody there. This is not a narrative about the victory of mercy, but a story of love reaching in two directions at once. Jesus' observation "Where did they all disappear to? Has no one condemned you?" can be read as a mere statement of fact. Or perhaps it is an ironic comment. Since Jesus knows they are sinners, he knows they will depart and he is feigning surprise. And then in mock reversal, he suggests that he will follow their compassionate example and not condemn the woman either. But perhaps he expected a different response from them. Perhaps when he exposed their own sinfulness, he expected them to stay and embrace the adulterous woman with the words, "My sister!" And perhaps, if we could peer into the heart of Jesus (which we cannot), he dreamed that she would embrace them back, "My brothers!" And he would take them all to his table of bread and wine and teach them to say, "Our Father!"

Perhaps the greatest story of the twin strategies for the twin hearts and the hope of reconciliation is the "man who had two sons" (Luke 15:11). The wayward son has created the classic script of the rejected heart. He knows he is worthless and he minces no words. "I have sinned against heaven and against you; I no longer deserve to be called your son. Treat me like one of your hired hands." The father's art of love is pure extravagance.

> While he was still far off, his father saw him and was
> filled with compassion; he ran and put his arms around
> him and kissed him.... "Quickly, bring out a robe—the
> best one—and put it on him; put a ring on his finger
> and sandals on his feet. And get the fatted calf and kill
> it, and let us eat and celebrate; for this son of mine was
> dead and is alive again; he was lost and is found!" (Luke
> 15:20–24).

The rejected heart that has cultivated its rejection comes to cherish itself as spurned. The only chance love has to penetrate this listless pity is abundant and overwhelming welcome.

The stay-at-home son speaks the classic script of the envious heart. "All these years I have been working like a slave for you, and I never disobeyed your command; yet you have never given me even a young goat so that I might celebrate with my friends." The older brother only knows who he is when he knows who his younger brother is not. The life of envy needs the rejection of others to flourish. The father holds up a mirror to his resentment. "Son, you are always with me, and all that is mine is yours." The older brother has lost nothing but the necessary foil for his self-righteousness. The final lines of the father are a second mirror to this anxious and oppressive heart. "But we had to celebrate and rejoice, because this brother of yours was dead and has come back to life; he was lost and has found." This is reminiscent of the unmasking question which closes the parable of the workers in the vineyard. "Am I not allowed to do what I choose with what belongs to me? Or are you envious because I am generous?" (Matthew 20:15).

I recently had the pleasure of telling this story of "A Man Who Had Two Sons" to a young woman who had never heard it before. She was a natural story listener and followed closely every nuance of the tale. When I finished, her first question was, "Did the older son go in?" I told her the story ends without telling us. Then I asked her, "Would you go in?" She did not speak for quite some time and then said, "I don't know. Would you?" I was about to flippantly reply, "Sure, I like parties," when the question of the heart and not social expectations hit me. Would I rejoice and party from my heart, forgive my brother from the heart? (Matthew 18:35). I thought for quite some time and said, "I don't know. Would you?"

Our hesitancy is not without precedent. The Gospels seem to indicate that Jesus' wholehearted welcome of the outcast produced wholehearted disgust on the part of the in-group. Jesus as banquet was received; Jesus as mirror was rejected. The total art of Jesus' love was to make the first last and the last first; so that all would be middle. It was to make the in out and out in; so that all would be together. It was to tell the ones who knew they were sinners that they were loved and to tell the ones who were loving themselves destructively that they were in sin. In this way both hearts could come together in their common need of repentance and their common openness to the free offer of divine love which Jesus was making available. This art of loving did not work. And it was not only that the envious heart decided not to join the feast; it decided to break the mirror. But before we look at the shattering of the mirror, we must explore further Jesus' total but differentiated offer of divine love.

The Rejected Heart Accepted

The electricity of Jesus' presence was that the love that flowed from him was free. It was given before the person was known and without soliciting promises of change. The source of the love was God; and although God wanted response and grieved when response was lacking, the lack of response did not stop the flow of love. This is a reversal of how things are usually done. The standard path of acceptance is: change your ways and we will accept you. This, in fact, was the structure of conversion in the Judaism of Jesus' day. The procedure was that the sinner was converted first and then became part of the community. Conversion first, communion second. "The novum in the act of Jesus was to reverse this structure: communion first, conversion second."[14] This freely available love, more than anything else, is the folly of God made manifest in Jesus.

The divine love of Jesus accepts us just because we are creatures, in spite of our failures that prove we are not worthy (the rejected heart) and in spite of our efforts to prove we are worthy (the envious heart). As James Mackey puts it, this type of forgiving love "had nothing to do with previous acts of contrition or promises of penance, much less with penance actually performed or sacrifices already made. It was the sense of our acceptance by God, not despite what we were, or because of what we were, but as we were."[15] This love tells the uninvited and unworthy, "Come eat with me!" And with that offer communicates the depth of love. This love tells the worthy, "You don't need all that to be loved!" And with that suggestion communicates the depth of love.

We are not accustomed to this. Upfront and unconditional love is not "the way the world works." We are trained in cautious and limited acceptance of ourselves and others. We know there are "things that make us good" and "things that make us bad." If we parade the good before others and bury the bad, we have a good chance of finding acceptance. On the other hand, if we are known by all to be bad and the very structure of society ratifies this judgment, then we can be assured the rejection we feel is "coming to us." What we do not expect is a love that cuts through these rather clear and common-sense regulations to embrace us at a level deeper than human thought and action. When this happens, the prized assumptions of our heart that makes us worthy and unworthy are called into question.

Jesus fell upon the obviously unworthy, not with pity for

their bereft lives or cunning allegiance with their sins, but with a call to act out the greatness of who they were. To stand before all that diminishes human life and bless those that are suffering it is an act of mind-boggling boldness. "Blessed are you poor...you who mourn...you who suffer...." Even if the blessedness is in light of a future vindication, it a present proclamation based on a perception of their inestimable value. To stand before those who have pretended to lose the desire for life and hype desire, "Seek! Ask! Knock!" is to love them in a way they cannot love themselves. But by far the best way to communicate this love is to gather them together in table fellowship. Their hearts are hungry, so feed them with so much bread and fish that there will be baskets left over. Their hearts are thirsty, so make more than enough wine to slake it. The abundance of the meals which Jesus hosted communicated God's overwhelming love to starved hearts. And when the banquet-giver had to leave, the way he wanted to be remembered was as bread that was more than itself and wine that was more than itself.

This message of divine acceptance communicated to the rejected heart certainly appears to be "good news." And the Gospels indicate that many welcomed it; and in the light of it, changed their lives. But there are also indications that there was resistance to this liberation from hidden self-hatred that Jesus brought. The simplest statement of the depth of sin is that we avoid with a passion the things that will save us. But this resistance to divine love is met by Jesus' persistence. Jesus is haunted by the agony of loss. The widow will hunt until she finds the lost coin; the shepherd will leave the many and search until he finds the strayed sheep; the father will run down one hill to meet the runaway and climb another hill to meet the one with no party in his heart. In order to catch the flavor and cost of communicating divine love to the rejected heart, we must tell a story.

Encounter at a Well

Those who have ears to hear, hear this story. Those who have eyes to see, see this scene. *Anything can happen at a well.*

The man who was sitting on the small stone ledge that circled the well slid off, turned to the woman who had just arrived, smiled and said, "I'm thirsty."

She had seen him at a distance. She had stopped to readjust the yoke which straddled her shoulders. A bucket hung from both ends of the yoke and when her steps were not perfect, and they seldom were, the wood cut into the flesh along the nape of her neck. She took the pain for granted, but from time to time she stopped to shift the weight to more calloused skin. From bruise to bruise, she thought. It was as she straightened from her bent posture, to gauge the last ground left before the well, that she saw him. He appeared to be waiting for her.

Her mind raced. She thought of turning around and making for the village. But if he wanted to, he could easily overtake her and take what he wanted. Then, she cursed. Why did she not come earlier in the day with the other women? She knew why. But right now that humiliation looked better than this danger. Then a plan formed out of her panic. She could see by his dress that he was a Jew and he would probably walk away. Most likely after some quick insult and with a great show of disdain. If not, she could make him go. She would steel herself, hide her mind, harden her heart. She knew how. She had been there before. It was not the first time.

"I'm thirsty," the man said again.

It was so blatant it took her back. At a distance she could manage him in her mind. Up close his presence was almost too much. But she recovered quickly. "Who isn't? This sun would fry a lizard's tongue."

"Give me a drink!"

"You—a Jew and a man—ask me—a Samaritan and a

woman—for a drink?" I have a simpleton on my hands she thought.

"Thirst makes friends of us all," the simpleton said. "I will help."

Before she could protest, he moved the lid off the top of the well; and stood waiting for her to give him the bucket.

"I'll do it," she said.

She let the bucket fall down the well. The splash rang up from below. She swung the rope sideways till the bucket at the bottom tipped and filled. Then with quick, successive jerks she pulled it to the top.

The man waited at her side. He said nothing.

If he thinks he is going to be first, she thought, he thinks wrongly. This is our well and it is my bucket. He will learn who he is here.

She rested the bucket on the ledge, hunched over it and splashed water toward her mouth. She drank like an animal that had been worked too long in the sun. All the time her eyes darted from the water to the silent man at her side. He was smiling. The simpleton has missed the meaning, she thought.

When she was done, she stepped back. The man did not move. She waited; then finally, jerked her arm toward the bucket. Slowly he cupped his hands, dipped them deep into the bucket, and brought the water to his mouth. As he drank, his face was turned up into the sun and the water ran and glistened in his beard. He drank like a bridegroom, loving the first cup of wedding wine.

With his lips still wet from the water the man turned to her. "If you would ask me, I would give you living water."

"The well is deep." Her tone was instructional. She felt as if she was giving a child a lesson in logic. "You do not have a bucket. Therefore, how do you propose to fetch this water?"

"Yokes and buckets are always the problem, aren't they?" said the man. His arms flew up in the air in exasperation.

A smile popped open her eyes; but her lips stayed tight and disapproving. Not a simpleton, she thought, a child. Just a child.

The child had a question. "Do you have a husband?"

The question slapped across her face. Not a child, she thought. A man, just another man. "I have no husband."

"True enough," said the man. "For you have had, ah, five husbands and the husband you have now is not your husband."

"Do you have a wife," she spat back.

"I have no wife," said the man.

"True enough," the woman said. "And the woman you had last night was not her either."

The man laughed, like someone had taken him and turned him upside down. He is enjoying this, she thought, but not for long.

"Besides, prophet, the number is not five but twelve."

"I was never good at numbers."

"One for each tribe of Israel," she said and thought that that would do it.

"Very pious of you," said the man. "Very pious."

This time she could not catch the laugh in her teeth and swallow it back. It escaped and howled out loud like a prisoner finally free in the sun.

"You are very hard to get rid of," she said; but now she wasn't sure whether she wanted him to go.

"Everyone says that," said the man.

One more try, she thought, and this Jew, like every other man, will surely leave me. "Tell me, O prophet who is not very good at numbers, where should we worship the living God? On the mountain or in the temple?"

The man grew silent and closed his eyes. He seemed to be traveling deep within himself to some sanctuary where she could not follow. So this is it, thought the woman. It will be in the name of the living God that he will spurn me. When the man opened his eyes, he caught hold of the woman's hand. "God is not on the mountain, but in your thirst. God is not in the temple but in the scream of your spirit; and it cries to me. Ask me, ask me for a drink."

Not just another man, she thought. Not just another man.

She pulled her hand back. "I don't ask." She said it like her whole life was in every word.

"Even without a bucket—if you ask me, I will give you living water."

So they sat on the ledge of the well under the sun which shines on good and bad alike. They spoke no words. Finally, he reached out for her hand. She let him take it.

"Give me a drink," she whispered.

"What," said the man, "you—a woman and a Samaritan—ask me—a Jew and a man—for a drink?"

"Thirst makes friends of us all," she said and smiled.

The man took her hands in his and formed them into a cup. Together their hands dipped deep into the bucket and brought a cradle of water to her lips. She drank it slowly, with her head back, her face open to the sky. She drank like a deer with the thirst of summer, like a field parched by drought, like a desert wanderer finally at home.

With her lips still wet she said to the man, "Sometimes the yoke and buckets cut into my flesh so bad I want to yell with pain; but I never do."

"I know."

Then she told him all about the husbands who were not husbands. She told him everything she ever did; everything she ever did she told him. All the time she spoke, she cried.

When she was finished, he said, "I know." Then he told back to her everything she ever did; everything she ever did he told back to her. All the time he spoke, he rubbed the nape of her neck where the marks of the yoke were the most punishing.

It was just as he had finished his revelation of her to herself that she saw the other men. His friends were coming toward them. "They will be scandalized to see me here with you." By now he held her in his arms.

"Probably," the man said.

"I must go." She eased out of his embrace and moved gracefully away from him. As she walked away, she turned often to look at him. Whenever she did, she always found him looking at her. Even when his companions gathered around him, he stood on the ledge of well and watched her go. Finally, she was so far away she could not watch him watching her.

Then she could not get to the village quickly enough. Once there, she went from house to house and told people about a man who was not just another man who taught her how to drink. It was only after she had stirred up the entire village that she realized she had left her yoke and buckets at the well and for the first time in memory she was not thirsty. The curious villagers formed a circle around her. She stood in the middle and proclaimed: "I met a man who told me everything I ever did—except how many times." And she laughed high and long. Some of the villagers said it sounded like she had a fountain of living water springing up inside her.

Let those who have ears to hear, hear this story. Let those who have eyes to see, see this scene. Anything can happen at a well.

⁙⧉⁙

The Envious Heart Unmasked

The envious heart prefers a love surrogate to the real affirmation that comes with the acceptance of divine love. The importance of this love surrogate has to be maintained; for if the surrogate itself is devalued in any way, it cannot confer self-worth. Therefore, a great deal of psychic energy goes into defending the glory and prestige of the surrogate. Also, a great deal of anger is unleashed when the surrogate is relativized in importance. But unless the "choke hold" on the love surrogate is loosened, the heart will never open onto a new grounding. The envious heart thinks that it possesses the love surrogate— wealth, righteousness, fame, and so on. But the truth is the surrogate possesses the heart. First, the heart must be freed from its addiction before it can move toward its creator.

The love that manifests itself in Jesus shows the heart in its actual situation. There can be no love without truth. Love always discloses the reality of the human condition. The love of Jesus that came as unexpected acceptance revealed the facade of the sinner. The loveless behavior was really a cry for love; the resignation to diminishment was really a hope for abundance. The love of Jesus which moves toward the envious heart will be no less revealing. This heart must see itself as it is before it can become anything else. The art of love that Jesus employed to open the eyes of the envious heart was both direct and indirect. The indirect strategy was to tell stories that overturned assumptions and offered an alternative way of being-in-the-world. The direct strategy was to shout out loud its distortion in the hope that those with ears would hear and those with eyes would see.

Paul Ricoeur suggests that the existential impact of the parables of Jesus can be appreciated in terms of orientation, disorientation, reorientation.[16] People construe the world and their role in it in a certain way. They then sort out their experiences in terms of this world-view. Along comes a story that this personally constructed world cannot make sense of. This disorients the hearers, forces them to look at the basic foundations of their life. But this does not lead to automatic reorientation. It leads to existential choice. The story does not so much shatter the world of the hearer as profoundly question it. If the question is accepted and pursued, new possibilities of living are disclosed. If the question is resisted, the construed world tightens and vigorously defends itself. The heart can see the kingdom yet fear the cost of entering it. "The light has come into the world, but people loved darkness rather than light" (John 3:19).

If it is the accident of birth that bestows worth on us and bestows disgrace on others, then listen to the story of the Good Samaritan (the disgraced other) and wonder. If wealth makes us somebody and poverty makes others nobody, listen to the story of Dives and Lazarus and wonder. If we pat ourselves on the back for fidelity and wag our finger at others for fickleness, listen to the story of the man with two sons and wonder. If it is hard work that has got us where we are and laziness that keeps others in their place, listen to the story of the workers in the vineyard and wonder. If it is our spotless purity that gives us a hearing before God and other people's sin that closes God's ears, then listen to the story of the tax collector and the Pharisee in the temple and wonder. If it is social position that makes you wanted and other people's lack of prestige that makes them abject, then listen to the story of the invited becoming uninvited and uninvited feasting at the banquet and wonder. The stories that Jesus told targeted the love substitutes and unmasked them as the anxious strivings and oppressive holdings of an envious heart.

Stories do not attack directly; they insinuate. They leave the hearers free to discover the criticism which is being directed at them. They are not a club over the head but a mirror to the heart. They allow the hearers to look at their falseness and destruction in a gentle and relatively nonthreatening way. In this sense, they are a wager on the wind. They are spoken and are over. Their full impact is never known. If they are effective, it is always with the participation of the hearers. Storytelling and story hearing are a cooperative venture. It is difficult to tell if a story hits home, if it is doing its religious work of uncovering the heart. Two reactions that are, in general, signals of effectiveness are exterior anger and interior musing. Both these responses usually mean the point, or at least a point, has been made. But stories often leave hearers befuddled. The story has had no impact; and the nonplussed hearers demand, "Speak plainly!" (John 16:29). If there was ever anyone who could speak plainly, it was Jesus.

What will you use today to bolster yourself at the expense of your brother and sister? Will it be lineage, glorying in the fact that you are a son of Abraham? God could raise up sons of Abraham out of these stones (Luke 3:8).

What will you use today to bolster yourself at the expense of your brother and sister? Will it be family? Unless you love me and the love I bring more than mother and father and brother and sister, you will not enter the kingdom of heaven (Mark 10:7).

What will you use today to bolster yourself at the expense of your brother and sister? Will it be your piety? Will you say long prayers in public places so that others will see you and whisper of your sanctity? Then go to the closet and pray there. And my Father who sees in secret will hear you (Matthew 6:4).

What will you use today to bolster yourself at the expense of your brother and sister? Will it be your wealth and inheritance? Then leave it all and follow me, for a camel has a better chance of passing through the eye of a needle then you do of entering the Kingdom of God (Mark 10:25).

What will you use today to bolster yourself at the expense of your brother and sister? Will it be your almsgiving? Will you pass your pennies to the blast of trumpets so all will know that you are a generous person? Then do not let your right hand know what your left hand is doing (Matthew 6:3).

What will you use today to bolster yourself at the expense of your brother and sister? Will it be your knowledge? Then become a child (Mark 10:15).

What will you use today to bolster yourself at the expense of your brother and sister? Will it be your power and authority? Then take this towel and wash the feet of the road-weary (John 13:1–11).

What will you use today to bolster yourself at the expense of your brother and sister? Will it be the dismal look on your face while you make known to all that you fast for the sins of others? Then comb your hair and smile, but inside starve (Matthew 6:16).

What will you use today to bolster yourself at the expense of your brother and sister? Will it be the honor you are held in? Then move from that first seat to the last (Luke 14:7).

You use everything you are and everything you have to strengthen yourself and weaken others. Give it up and the kingdom will be yours!

Indirect storytelling and direct confrontation was the art of how Jesus loved the envious heart. Both of these activities were mirror operations. But the deeper unmasking reality was the person of Jesus himself. He came at life out of an inner fullness which exposed their inner emptiness. He would not grasp at the things they thought conferred significance and he would not grovel in the lack of life or spread destruction like the rejected. He was the free spirit whom those in chains either admire and follow or loathe and kill. In the last analysis, it was the freedom of Jesus that made him intolerable.

We told a story of how God's love in Jesus pursued a rejected heart. We need a story of how God's love in Jesus pursues an envious heart. It is told in the first person by *a man who once met Jesus.*

❖

The Jesus I Knew

My mind wanders off more now. It is like a child who has strayed from the safety of his father's hand and is running through a meadow of flowers intent on something in the distance. Every so often the child looks back at me to see if he should go on. And I am torn between issuing a stern parental order to return or following him to some wondrous discovery. I cannot do either and I begin to wonder what is wrong with me. It is then that the child fades; and I see Jesus again, turning, forever turning, never turning away and never turning back.

That is why I have come to this deserted olive grove and sit with my back against the bark of this ancient tree. Its leaves shield me from the heat and the sky filtered through the branches is strangely calming. I need time alone to sort things out. Even my friends agree.

Just yesterday at a meal which I hosted, with Levi and Benjamin bantering in argument the way I love it, my mind suddenly unmoored from the debate and drifted back to Jericho. I was inside myself again, going over what happened, piecing it together like a potter trying to mend a pot. Then the background buzz of the conversation died down; and I came back to the faces around the table. They were staring at me.

"Bored, Nathaniel?" Benjamin said.

"Sorry."

"The man of one thousand opinions has nothing to say? What has happened to that famous razor mind of yours? Gone dull?"

"Cutting elsewhere," I mumbled. "Cutting myself," I thought.

"Like last week in court," Benjamin snapped.

"Benjamin! Let's not go over it again." It was Levi's usual suggestion. Avoidance.

"No. He needs to hear it."

So he told me. I did not need to hear it. I already knew. In court I was unfolding what I thought to be the core of the case, what more and more I see as the core of everything—how God, the law, and human frailty are locked in an eternal embrace. We love the law for it is the only hope of a weak people. But the holy law we love only whispers to us that we are unholy. And God remains God. Unapproachable. The judge interrupted me.

"The application, please."

"What?"

"The application. We all know everything in Israel is based on God's law." He was telling me I was tedious. "And we thank you for reminding us." Not only tedious, but arrogant. "But the question is the connection? Where are you going with all this?"

So I followed my mind—run, child, run—discovering connections as I went, growing excited at what I was finding. Then I became afraid like a deer who leaves the hills for water and suddenly finds lions by the pool. I wound down, hoping the connection was somewhere in all the words I had spoken. I looked around for the nodding heads and appreciative faces. Heads were bowed; faces studied the floor.

"Undoubtedly," replied the judge who was now visibly annoyed. "But the case before us has to do with the division of an inheritance." His voice was insistent; his finger was jabbing a message at me. "We will take it up again tomorrow when we are all better prepared."

"Unprepared!" Benjamin's voice broke into my own remembering. "Well, it's not all that bad. More embarrassing than anything else, I suppose." That was Benjamin's way, make it harsh then take it back, hit then console. "But it doesn't do your reputation any good. Some are saying this sudden—what is it Nathaniel, looseness? drifting?—in you is because of that debate with the Galilean teacher."

"It wasn't a debate."

"Take my, no, take all of our advice. Forget him." Levi said nothing. He agreed.

"How?"

"You are a lawyer. Think it through. Make it work for you. Turn it around."

Benjamin was right. That is the only way. And that is why with this tree at my back to steady me, I am going over it again. I know how it will end. With Jesus turning, forever turning, never turning away and never turning back. But maybe by the time I get to him turning, I will find something new and know what to do.

It started when Caiaphas sent for me. Many knew about it. I made sure of that. I just told Simeon that I would be late for our appointment because the high priest wanted to see me. Simeon was owed the courtesy of an explanation; and he could be counted on to tell others.

When I entered his chambers, Caiaphas was alone. That was unusual. I took it as an honor to me and that our meeting was important. He began by saying that he had heard of me, and even though I was a young man I had "already distinguished myself" as a lawyer. He was obviously referring to the case of the priest Jude.

Jude had a reputation for being pious. At dawn and dusk he could be seen praying in the temple. The pilgrims always quieted down and pointed at him as they passed by. But according to the accusation, between these times of pious prayer he had been reselling the animals which the pilgrims had brought to the temple for sacrifice. He would accept the offerings but would never offer them. Instead he would sell them to other pilgrims who were looking for atonement sacrifices. The specific charge was that he sold the same goat five times. There were many witnesses to this double dealing and they came forward, outraged and scandalized, and pointed their righteous arms at him all the time they spoke.

First, I gathered testimony from his fellow priests as to Jude's sanctity. One was more eloquent than the next. When they were done, Jude was the holiest Jew next to Moses. Then I cited the famous saying of the Honored Rabbi Hananish. "No man denies the derivatives unless he had previously denied the Root." If one breaks the commandments, it is because one has broken with God himself. The argument flowed: If Rabbi Hananish is correct, the reverse is also true. No man in touch with the Root, can deny the derivatives. If the sanctity of Jude has been attested to, can his moral righteousness be doubted? Can a man in contact with God break God's law? The iron logic bound the judge. Jude was acquitted. My name became known.

I had "already distinguished myself" by saving a priest, and the high priest had taken note. "I have a mission for you, Nathaniel. You have heard of the Teacher from Galilee, Jesus. We need more information about him. He is now beyond the Jordon in Bethany with friends of his. He is preaching there. Go, observe what he has to say and report back." I had heard that was the way it was with Caiaphas, direct with always hints of more.

That night I told my wife that Caiaphas had said that even though I was a young man I had "already distinguished myself" as a lawyer. The next day she told the other wives. That night they told their husbands. And the next day I could sense a new respect in the street for me. The greetings seemed a little more respectful; the other lawyers seemed a little more eager for me to notice them. It worked.

It was not hard to find Jesus in Bethany. Everyone on the road seemed to be moving toward the house of Lazarus. When I got there he was teaching. I thought it best not to hide myself, but to become part of the crowd and sit like the others. One more Jew come to learn. Of course my clothes obviously spoke of position and importance. But I would let the people whisper their own conclusions later. Never show too much.

His message seemed mainline enough. It was about retribution, about the way sin subtly entraps the sinner. He knew the teachings of the rabbis and he had a way with words. For his finale he twisted the great Elazar. "For by the measure with which you measure, it will be measured back to you." The customary silence was on us all, allowing the teaching to sink in. Finally, a choked voice, old and oozing urgency, spoke up.

"But, Teacher, what is the measure?"

Jesus lit up. His arms began to tear at the air like he was pulling treasure from it. "The kingdom of God is like a poor woman in the marketplace. She carries her few coins in a purse which hangs from a string around her neck. If anyone wants the coins, he will have to take her head as well." We all laughed. We knew her well.

"She has her basket with her; sackcloth is tied all around the inside. She will lose none of the wheat she has come to buy. She is determined to get her full measure. No merchant will cheat her. As the seller fills her basket, she shakes the wheat together to make sure it settles tightly. But she does not stop at that. She then presses it down with her hands and forearms so more can fit. She will get all that is coming to her." They all nodded. They had been there.

"When suddenly under the pressure of her pressing, the wheat reverses. What was pushed down, pushes up. The basket becomes a fountain of wheat, running over into her lap. It shows no signs of stopping and the last we see of her, she is up to her waist in wheat. Both her purse and bushel basket are lost. That is the measure."

I remember the looks on the faces of the people. Some sat in stunned silence; some were laughing; some were laughing and crying the way people sometimes do when the long-hoped-for happens before their eyes; some walked away to be by themselves. They all seemed to be moved by the story, to understand it instantly.

But I was confused. Wheat can't bubble like water. A child's fantasy. It made no sense. So I did what I was sent to do. I observed.

When I reported to Caiaphas, I made the mistake of keeping the story for last, adding it as an afterthought with the comment that it seemed a simple diversion. For a long time he weighted me on the scales of his eyes. Then he turned and with his back to me he spoke. "He is insinuating that there is no measure; and the careful, studied way of life of which we are the guardians must give way to this enthusiasm. The target of this diversion in case you missed it, my distinguished lawyer, is us." I remember the rush of shame. It was like I was a little boy who had to be told the importance of things.

"But you are right about one thing," Caiaphas turned back toward me. "Stories are of little help to us. We need a clear confrontation, a stubborn statement of his mind. He needs to be tested."

"I can do it." I never thought about the words. They were just there. I needed to prove myself in Caiaphas' eyes, to find my true weight on those scales.

"Good. I will send for you." And he left the room.

I thought it would be soon, but it wasn't. Still, no day passed that I did not hope that he would ask for me. I wanted to redeem myself.

Finally, the word came. When I arrived to see him, he was with Annas and two other priests. They never left the room as we talked.

"Jesus is in Jericho," Caiaphas began without introducing me. "From our reports," he widened his arms to include his fellow priests, "it seems he has come out in the open. Less stories, more direct speech. He needs to be skillfully pushed, and he will say the intemperate words we know are in his heart. Push him for us, Nathaniel."

"Yes." Exactly what I had hoped for.

From Jerusalem to Jericho is always a dangerous trip. Thieves love its twists and turns. But on the way down my head was too busy with strategies to worry. I imagined every possible scenario and walked through each one a victor. I tested him, showed him up for what he was, and justified myself; and with me all who stood for the law. On the way down I did not give danger a thought for all my thoughts were on the contest to come.

On the way back the worst had already happened.

I found him in the small valley outside the city. There were about a hundred people around him. I remembered I wished there were more. The moment he stopped his preaching I stepped forward. There would be no being one of the crowd this time.

"Teacher," I began. Always honey before vinegar, the kiss before the slap. "What must I do to gain eternal life?" Sincere questions are the best test. I remembered the poignancy of "Master, what is the measure?"

He was in no hurry to respond. He looked at me for a long time. I forced myself to return his stare. I never looked down.

"What does the law say?"

Clever, I thought, the tester tested. He knows the game. I will show him.

In the purest tones I recited.

> Love the Lord, your God,
> With your whole mind,
> With your whole heart,
> With your whole soul.
> And your neighbor
> As yourself.

Approval rippled across the crowd. It pleased me.

He spread his arms out, signaling to me to receive the

recognition of the people, nodding to himself all the time. "You have answered well. Do this and live."

Then there was silence again between us. I had been tested and had justified myself. But there had to be more. No one had won.

"Who is my neighbor?" It was a question worth a week of arguments, but it showed too much. The people stirred. The sincere seeker was now unmasked as the heresy hunter. A slight smile danced around Jesus' mouth.

He came across to where I stood. He grabbed both my shoulders, steadying me on my feet, squaring me off like he was readying me for a blow. He locked my eyes into his.

"A certain man went down from Jerusalem to Jericho," he began. He did not go on until he saw in my eyes that I knew I was that man. Then he moved away from me to tell everyone what happened to me on that journey.

The first blow was the easiest to take. Being left for dead is not dead. Skin heals. I would mend. I still had clothes and money and prestige in Jerusalem. All I needed was to get back there.

A priest on a donkey came by. I could barely make him out. The blood was crusting over my eyes. But even naked he recognized me. "Nathaniel, is that you?" I had no strength to speak. I could not even move my hands to signal him.

"O my God!" The priest held his head. "You, of all people, will understand. I have just finished service in the temple. If I touch you and you are already dead or if you die in my arms, I will be ritually impure." He paced back and forth on the road above me, hunched in thought and panic.

"They will force me to stand in shame at the Eastern gate, and go through the long process of purification. It would be a scandal to myself, my household, and the priesthood." He rose to his full height and did not look at me. "In this case, as you well know, the law entitles me to pass by." I watched him go. He took with him more than the thieves had taken.

A Levite came next. As soon as he saw me, he jumped off the road down into the ditch. "Thieves," the hoarse sound came from deep within his chest. He looked quickly around, but not at me. In my heart I yelled, "Help!" He never heard it. He stayed low in the ditch and when he was sure the thieves were no longer lurking about, he returned, running, to the road.

I now had nothing, so nothing came to me. Even through the blood I could see he was a Samaritan. But in his eyes were my tears.

The damnable thing about it was that it took so long. If only he would have cursed, thrown me on his animal, dropped me in a heap at an inn and went his way with a slur, "More than you would have done for me." But he cleaned me like a mother bathes a child, rubbed oil in my wounds, tore his own robe for bandages. He put me on his donkey and walked beside it, steadying me. At the inn he put me on a cot and placed his blankets over me. I could hear him paying the innkeeper and saying he would be back to take care of me if it was needed. All that time, that endless time, he never spoke to me. Except for the tears.

The next thing I knew Jesus had me by the shoulders again. He, too, had my tears in his eyes. "Who proved neighbor to the one in need?" It was the only question I have ever heard that was not a test.

And for once I just spoke, not worrying right from wrong, not breathless for approval. I uttered sounds that were not recitation. My sounds, halting, like a child speaking for the first time. "The one who showed mercy."

"You," and the place inside me that just spoke heard the word.

"Go," and it was like an invitation to a feast.

"And do the same," and I found tears in my eyes but I did not know for whom I cried.

Then he began to turn; and that is how I always see him.

Turning, forever turning, never turning away and never turning back.

The next day I returned to Jerusalem. I went immediately to see Caiaphas. His chamberlain came out to meet me in the antechamber. "The high priest has asked me to tell you that he has already been told about what happened."

At my house Benjamin was waiting. "I heard it was quite a battle but ended in a standoff."

"It was not a battle."

"I heard he cleverly changed your question and you cleverly slipped out of having to say the Samaritan was neighborly."

"At the time there were no Samaritans. Or Jews. Or Gentiles. Or priests. Or lawyers. Only those who cry and those who pass by." That was the beginning of my thinking about it, of trying to understand what happened.

I'm still at it. In this deserted olive groove, with my back against this tree, under this luminous sky it all comes back to me. I know now it is not over. My wounds have not healed. Perhaps they are not supposed to. The cost of my healing is still going on. So I know he will come back for me. He said he would.

❧ ☙

Crucified

The lawyer of the story is struggling. He has opened himself to the experience of Spirit and is gradually being transformed by it. But Jesus was not so successful with others. The truth he held up for the envious heart to see did not make it repentant, but turned it to stone. Divine love in Jesus moved toward both hearts at once; but the historical records seem to say that this love was received by the lowly and the sinners and rejected by the powerful and the self-righteous. But this fact should not lead us to facile judgments about the openness of the rejected heart. It would be too one-sided to characterize the envious heart as entrenched and the rejected heart as receptive. Self-hatred and self-importance are equally resistant to the new grounding which divine love offers.

But the Gospels do stress the endless machinations of the envious heart. The moment the rejected reached toward the love of God in Jesus, the envious turned their back. The welcome extended to sinners was an immediate insult extended to them. They perceived themselves as pure and would not join the table fellowship with those they perceived as impure. To share bread was to share peace, trust, and life; and to share bread with everyone was to blur the boundaries between right and wrong, good and bad. More to the point, it was to break down the cherished structure of righteous division and to suggest a common creaturehood, equally sinful and equally capable of redemption. There was a more appropriate response to Jesus than to eat with him and his friends. "The Pharisees went out and immediately conspired with the Herodians against him, how to destroy him" (Mark 3:6).

The exact path of this plotting and who was involved is difficult to trace. The Romans most probably cooperated with the execution of Jesus because they thought he claimed a political messiahship. "King of the Jews" is a seditious title, and that is the charge tacked to the cross. From the religious side the death of Jesus is pursued because he is perceived as violating God's law. He is a blasphemer (Mark 2:7), in league with Beelzebub (Mark 3:22), a violator of the Sabbath (Luke 13:10–17), and a false prophet (Mark 14:65). His cleansing of the temple (Mark 11:15–19) shows his disrespect for the spiritual and moral center of Judaism and his association with sinners shows his disregard for the law. But however the death of Jesus is construed, one factor should not be forgotten. In the last analysis, the death of Jesus is a theological murder.

From a highly developed Christian theological viewpoint, it is the sin of the world which kills Jesus. But from the point of view of the religious authorities of Jesus' day, God's law orders Jesus' death. A divine command is behind the whole thing. The validation of the plot to do away with Jesus is a certain understanding of God and how he deals with his creatures. His death is pursued in the name of one God; and he goes to his death in the name of another God. The utterly transcendent God whose law is absolute and unyielding condemns him; Abba who whispers in his ear affirms him. It is the depth of sin that murdered the love of God in Jesus. But the depth of sin is a lie about the nature of God.

In chapter three of Genesis, the serpent lies about the divine intention. God is not the endless lover of created life, but only the subtlest of self-seekers. He has forbidden the eating of the fruit to protect his own power. "No," says the snake, "You will not die; for God knows that when you eat of it your eyes will be opened, and you will be like God, knowing good and evil" (Genesis 3:4–5). This God that is defensive of himself and oppressive of others is the projection of sinful human instincts. God is like us, only stronger. This God ratifies human alienation and justifies the divisive behavior of his followers. It is this God, enthroned in the rejected and envious hearts of his followers, who wants the blood of Jesus. The other name for this God is the one who first told the earth couple of his existence—Satan. The lie about God in the human heart seeks to kill the truth about God in Jesus.

This perspective is important to maintain. When the story of Jesus reaches its final stages in the arrest, trial, and crucifixion, the focus often shifts from Jesus and other people to Jesus and his relationship to God. Will Jesus abandon his faith and "curse God and die"? Will God intervene on Jesus' behalf and save him from the hands of his foes? The drama is being played out on the level of transcendent relationships. This is a

necessary plot development. The Christian sensitivity that produced the passion narratives was convinced that the cross was
the supreme moment of revelation. The relationship between
the father and the son and, by extension, between God and
humankind was being disclosed. But it must be remembered
that the death of Jesus "is your hour, and the power of darkness!" (Luke 22:53). To forget this is to become ethereal and
remove the cross from the conflicts of history. Whatever is
happening between Jesus and God is happening because the
sin of the human heart is in the ascendancy. The cross of Jesus
is first and always but never exclusively horror.

In the resurrection of Christ, the truth about God van-
quished the lie about God. God raises Jesus from the dead and
thereby validates his life and message. The ultimate trustworthy Abba who grounds all creation is indeed trustworthy. What
appeared to be defeat has been turned into victory. This simple
contrast was probably the earliest interpretation of the resurrection. "Let it be known to all of you, and to all the people of
Israel, that this man is standing before you in good health by
the name of Jesus Christ of Nazareth, whom you crucified,
whom God raised from the dead....They put him to death by
hanging him on a tree, but God raise him up on the third day..."
(Acts 4:10; 10:40). God vindicates Jesus, and in doing so reveals the truth about himself. He is not the plotting God behind the death of Jesus. He is the God ahead of Jesus, opening
up for him a new and transformed existence.

But the simple proclamation of vindication is not adequate
enough to interpret the complex experience of Jesus' death
and resurrection. Too much is left unanswered. Is the cross,
then, only something that happened on the road to glory?
Granted that it is a sign of the depth of human sinfulness, is
that all it is? Is there a neat division between the death and the
resurrection—the death revealing sin and the resurrection revealing love? In meditating on the death of Jesus in the light of

the resurrection and with the aid of the Hebrew Scriptures, new understandings of the cross emerged. The death of Jesus was seen to fit into a divine plan. It was not merely the temporary frustration of divine purposes, but it was necessary for the accomplishment of salvation. "Was it not necessary that the Messiah should suffer these things and then enter into his glory?" (Luke 24:26). This is the infamous "divine must" of the crucifixion. Simple contrast between death and resurrection yields to a sense of continuity. The God who raised Jesus was also, mysteriously, involved in his death.

This mysterious involvement of God in the death of Jesus is further explored in the light of Isaiah and the myth that the death of a just man atones for sins. "But he was wounded for our transgressions, / crushed for our iniquities; / upon him was the punishment that made us whole, / and by his bruises we are healed" (Isaiah 53:5). This passage connects the death of Jesus with sin in a new way. Sin remains the secret energy of the plot against Jesus and his ultimate executioner. But a reversal, so favored in the parables of Jesus, has been envisioned. In the very act of the sinful heart rejecting divine love, divine love has healed the sinful heart. This interpretation links the death of Jesus with his entire mission. His whole life was the mediation of divine love to human sinfulness. Now the cross is seen to be the place where that mediation was most powerfully present. Not only is the cross the result of sin, it is the event that heals sin. The cross now cuts two ways. It reveals the human resistance to divine love and the divine persistence in soliciting human love.

The interpretation of the death of Jesus has come full circle. It began as a tragedy about the triumph of evil; and, in the light of the resurrection, the experience of the Spirit, and meditation on the Hebrew Scriptures, it has become a comedy about the outpouring of divine love. Each gospel reflects the conviction that the death of Jesus is a statement about God. In Matthew, the earth quakes, boulders split, and tombs open. These are signs of a theophany, an unveiling of God. In Mark, the temple curtain which hides the divine presence is ripped in two and the centurion proclaims, "Clearly this man was the Son of God." God is now out in the open for all to see. In Luke, the crucified Jesus offers divine forgiveness to his executioners and hands his spirit over to his Father. His death is more a time of faith than of terror. In John, the last words of the dying Jesus are "Now it is finished." The cross ties up the work of the Word-Made-Flesh rather than fundamentally threatening it. The truth about God not only asserted itself in the rising of Christ; it was also manifest in the dying of Jesus.

The early followers of Jesus scratched crosses on walls and medallions, forged iron and tied sticks in cruciforms, and gathered around tables to break bread so they would not forget his broken body and drink wine so they would not forget his outpoured blood. The centuries of humdrum liturgies have dulled us to the radical nature of this activity. Time has tamed both its oddity and novelty. Why take the cross of Jesus as the sign of faith and eat a meal in the memory of his death? The central proclamation was that love brings life out of death. The catalytic experience was the resurrection. Without that experience, as Saint Paul says, faith would be in vain; and Jesus would have been forgotten, one more mutilated body in the history of "dumb suffering." The image of it all should surely be the glorified Christ. Ultimately there was victory. Why not take Jesus at the right hand of the Father as the "compressed picture" of faith? In the interest of theological accuracy, it would seem a different image should have been chosen.

Practical reasons would reinforce this. The cross was a symbol of execution, a punishment reserved for enemies of the state. To follow the way of the cross would be to advertise yourself as a threat to established authorities. But more than that, the sight of a cross immediately produced repulsion. It carried the feel of death, not as a natural end to long life, but as the brutal and arbitrary intrusion of power. It was the most concrete reminder imaginable of the fragility of human life and the oppressive threat that each person is to every other. Would people be attracted to a symbol that was geared to evoke terror? If apologetics or proselytizing urged the early Christians to adopt the symbol of the cross, it was a poor strategy indeed.

The reason for the centrality of the cross is that somehow it said it all. It captured the experience of Spirit in all its uniqueness and power. The cross articulates the interactive flow that characterizes the God-person relationship. This is the ultimate Mystery of Christian faith and it is not reducible to a single insight. In Tillich's language, it is not an accidental mystery which can be solved; but it is an essential mystery which, the more it is known, the more mysterious it becomes. Our hope is to explore it in the light of the rejected and envious heart and so connect it to Jesus' overall concern. In order to do this, we must pursue the ancient question that is the instant overflow of contact with Jesus, "What think ye of the Christ?"

The experience of the risen Christ forced the question of Jesus' identity with new urgency. From the first moment of his ministry "who Jesus was" was the question lurking behind the tumult of events. But Jesus seemed reluctant to address his own identity except in relationship to the kingdom of God. His interest was in what God was doing in human life and how he and other people should respond. As we discussed in the first chapter, "who he was" was the ultimate grounding for "what he was doing"; but what "he was doing" was so fascinating that it was getting all the time and attention. With the resurrection the emphasis shifts from Jesus' saving presence to his personal identity. In Bultmann's famous phrase, "The proclaimer becomes the One Proclaimed."

The articulation of Jesus' identity is an extremely complex

development. In many ways it will be the abiding concern of the Church for the first five centuries. It will achieve, not closure, but stability at the Council of Chalcedon in 451. In this process the image that will emerge as the most provocative revelation of his mystery will be "Son of God." The resurrection experience brings Jesus' ultimate reality "into the clear"; but it does not confer an identity on Jesus that he did not have prior to his rising from the dead. In the Spirit-guided reflection of the early Church there seems to be a steady retrogression. Jesus is the Son, not only at the resurrection but on the cross; not only on the cross, but at the baptism; not only at the baptism, but from birth; not only at birth, but from all eternity. The life, death, and resurrection of Jesus of Nazareth is the life, death, and resurrection of the Son of God. From this perspective Jesus is not only the revelation of humanity in relationship to God but also the revelation of God in relationship to humanity.

With Jesus' identity established as Son of God, a high Christology is firmly in place. In mythological language, it is now the fullness of time when "Son of God will become man" and "the Word will become flesh." It is often pointed out that the problem of all high Christologies is that the humanity of Jesus suffers. In the downward movement of God to humanity, Son and Word never quite make it. The Son almost becomes man; the Word almost becomes flesh. This is certainly the major danger of articulating the event of Jesus Christ in the images of "Son" and "Word." But there is also a major advantage to this approach. From the perspective of religious experience, salvation is always inaugurated by the divine. The human person is a receiver and a responder to the divine initiative. When the life, death, and resurrection of Jesus is appreciated as a "top down" movement, we keep this experiential dynamic in the forefront. In the next chapter, Jesus of Nazareth stretched on the cross will tell us something about the perils of human response; but in this chapter the Son of God stretched on the cross tells us something about the perils of divine love.

But it must be stated that the cross as a revelation of God does not replace the cross as a revelation of sin. In the Gospel accounts, the two are held in tension. This juxtaposition focuses the twin elements of the experience of Spirit—divine love and human sinfulness. The literary device used to maintain this tension is irony. The passion and death in the Gospel of John is a masterpiece of irony; but all the gospels deal ironically with Jesus' death. In John, Caiaphas proposes the advantage of having one man die for the people. The hearers know that it is Caiaphas' envious heart that generates this proposal; but they also know this is true in a way Caiaphas does not surmise. In Luke, the soldiers mock Jesus by placing the inscription THIS IS THE KING OF THE JEWS over his head; but they do not know they are telling the truth. In Mark, the priest and scribes jeer: "He saved others but he cannot save himself. Let the 'Messiah,' the 'king of Israel,' come down from the cross here and now so that we can see it and believe in him!" But the hearers know that it is in Jesus' staying on the cross that salvation comes. Matthew adds to these insults the taunt, "After all, he claimed, 'I am God's Son.'" But it is precisely as God's Son that he remains on the cross. What is this irony intended to convey?

In the crucifixion of Jesus, the Son of God, human sinfulness is at the height of its powers. It is raging out of control. Jesus' friends have deserted him, the mob has turned against him, the religious authorities have engineered his crucifixion and mock him, the soldiers torture him, and the state condemns him. The demonic has broken loose. Satan has entered not only the heart of Judas but also the heart of the world. Yet this marshaled campaign of evil against divine love is subverting itself. It is attempting to kill the Son of God; and its very success will be its downfall. The wholehearted (rejected and envious) explusion of divine love will establish it as ultimate truth of human life. In imagistic language, the cross of agony becomes the throne of glory. Or in the developed reflection of the Johannine Christ, "And I, when I am lifted up from the earth, will draw all people to myself" (John 12:32). How is this possible?

It may be a wicked and adulterous generation that asks for a sign that tests the love of God; but, as so often in the past, God will provide a sign. But it will not be a sign that ratifies the rejected heart in its worthlessness or the envious heart in its righteousness. They will receive a sign but not the sign their sinfulness craves. The Gospel of Mark is carefully constructed so that the reader or hearer is led to the true sign which God offers. In Mark, there is the phenomenon of the messianic secret. The devils are orthodox; they know Jesus is the Son of God. But every time they shout out his identity, he silences them. When Jesus heals the deaf and the blind, he forbids the new ears and new eyes to reveal what has happened. Mark is afraid that these exorcisms and miracles will be taken as the "much-requested" sign. Although the Son of God has the power to spectacularly overturn the work of Satan, he is not revealed in that power. The Son of God is revealed in the power to die.

The Tested Heart

An illuminating way to explore this faith conviction that the love of God is revealed in the willingness to die is to process it through the "testing" tradition. This tradition has a long and winding history, but for our purposes two perspectives are helpful.[17] First, the truth of relationships is only known through the trials that test them. If the relationship undergoes no difficulties, the fidelity of the partners is always in question. In the Hebrew Scriptures, Yahweh tests people to find out if they love him. He tests his covenant son, King Hezekiah, "to know all that was in his heart" (2 Chronicles 32:31). After the successful testing of Abraham, Yahweh concludes, "Now I know…" (Genesis 22:12). This is an experiential truth of all relationships. Once they have survived difficult times, the bonding is more intimate and the people involved know one another more deeply and trust one another more thoroughly. The harsh truth seems to be that trials successfully undergone strengthen relationships, because they expose the hearts of the people involved.

Second, sin is the source of the testing between God and people; and the successful completion of the test strips the tester of its power. The thoroughgoing monotheism of the Hebrew Scriptures cannot imagine anything outside of divine control. Therefore, the trials that tested the people's faith in the covenant were seen to be sent by God to find out "what was in the heart." A later development of this theme saw Yahweh sending Satan to play the role of tester. The Book of Job is the classic example of this dynamic. By New Testament times, Satan appears to be working on his own. Satan can never be envisioned as completely outside God's power for that would come dangerously close to the heresy of dualism. Two coequal principles, one good and the other evil, battling over the world. But neither is Satan God's obedient servant. In the Gospels, Satan does not seem to be on a divine leash. He appears to be, as Cyril of Jerusalem described him, a dragon who sits by the side of the road seeking whom he may devour.

This development is extremely important. When Yahweh was imaged as a tester, he was not far from a tyrant. On the one hand, he afflicts his most faithful of servants in order to satisfy his slightest doubt. He appears as an insecure lover, continually putting up obstacles to see if he is really loved. On the other hand, he allows no testing of himself. Although the creature was always accountable, God was never to be questioned.

The prohibition against putting God to the test reveals an important element in the Old Testament conception of Jaweh's covenant relationship with his people. The reciprocal promises and obligations do not have to be balanced out and accounted; indeed, the concept of God's covenant obligation is in the last resort an irrational one, losing itself eventually in the inscrutability of the all-holy, sovereign God.[18]

This way of dealing admirably maintains the transcendence of God; but over a long period of time, we question whether this covenant is a loving one. The thundering voice from the whirlwind may silence Job momentarily; but it does not shut him up forever.

It is theologically possible to see the relationship between God and his people being tested by sin. Neither partner seeks a testing. Temptation is not to be played with; it is truly a threat to the relationship and could destroy it. But temptations and trials are inevitable. Sin is deeply embedded in the human condition, and its principle work is to disturb the creator-creature relationship. This double sentiment of not wanting the test but knowing it will arrive is succinctly expressed in the ending of Matthew's version of the Our Father: "And do not bring us to the time of trial, / but rescue us from the evil one" (Matthew 6:13). Also, in this understanding, sin tests both partners in the relationships. It tests the love of God for humanity, and it tests the love of people for God and for one another. Sin is the enemy of both God and humanity. Against this background the cross as the sign of divine love is illuminated.

The death of the Son of God is the testing of divine love by the sinful human heart. The sinful heart that Jesus encounters does not believe the message of divine love. The rejected heart has waited so long for the one who does not come that when at last he comes, he is not accepted. It would rather live in cynical rage at the fact it is spurned than to receive the burden of significance. The envious heart has tried to please for so long and was not able that it has come to love its own standards of pleasing. It will not receive the other-centered love that will free it, for it has learned to love the self-centered love that imprisons it. The school of sin educates us in fear and teaches us to maintain the lovelessness we have learned to love. The Son of God has offered the love of the Father, but who can believe it? It needs to be tested. And the arena of testing should be the place where we are most sure we are not loved.

It is death which panics the heart and tells us it is worthless. From the shaken and unsure center of the person comes the strategies of rejection and envy. If divine love is to radically reconcile the person, it must encounter the terrorized heart. The basis of these terrors may be rooted in our finitude, in the natural death that flows from birth. But human mortality is a "relatively neutral" foundation compared to the destruction people have erected on it. Death is most terrifying when it is inflicted on us by our fellow human beings. What we fear most is desertion by our friends and being handed over to our enemies. It is the fear of this abandonment and the loneliness and humiliation of this perishing that convicts us that we are nothing. This type of death, then, becomes the test of the love of God mediated through his Son.

When the Son of God died on the cross, the test was successfully passed; and the power of the tester, the sinful heart, was broken. In its place the liberated heart lives in the paradoxes of God. "What died upon the cross was death." "In his dying we are reborn." "Sin killed the Son of God and was, in turn, killed by the Son of God." "We soiled our hands with the blood of Christ and it cleansed them." "We crucified Love and Love raised us from the dead." The cross of the Son of God is the final, and most powerful, mediation of divine love to human sinfulness. The life of the Son of God tried to embrace the panicked heart and was, on the whole, tentatively received. The death of the Son of God broke through this rejection and envy in a new and ingenious way. God died the death we fear; and so freed us from the fear of death. Sin runs deep in us; and the only love we will believe is the love that lays down its life. It is the only love we can be sure we did not make up.

It goes on still. As long as we wait and do not know the one we wait for has come; as long as we strive, deceive, and oppress and do not know we do not have to, the Son of God stays on the cross. He stays there because to come down would be to ratify the inner energy of our sin and leave us unredeemed. He stays there so that the hardness of our hearts will encounter the outpouring of divine love. He stays there so we will not settle for the world as it is, but continue to ask the question of redemption which his cross, forever concrete and unyielding, focuses: "In vain, my Christ, in vain, two thousand years have gone by and men crucify you still. When will you be born, my Christ, and not be crucified any more, but live among us for eternity?"

For Further Reflection

1. Point out examples from current events of a "rejected heart" and an "envious heart."
2. Explain the paradox of love as the source of power.
3. Dialogues between God and the heart are a traditional form of religious expression. Here is an example:

    > *God:* I made you and I love you.
    > *Heart:* You have a strange way of showing it.
    >   If you love me, make me like you.
    >   Immortal. Above it all.

God: I love you as mortal.
Heart: But I do not love myself that way.
  I hide from it day and night.
God: I will join you in the brightness of day
  and the darkness of night.
Heart: In the brightness of day maybe.
God: And in the darkness of night.
Heart: As you?
God: No. As you. I will send my Son.
Heart: You will back off.
  You will not hand him over.
  You do not know the terror.
God: But I know you and I love you.
  Where you are I want to be.
Heart: But I don't want to be where I am.
God: When I am there,
  we will go through it together;
  we will not lose love.
Heart: You will not go through it.
  You will play God and run.
  Take me with you.
God: I would rather be with you
  so that you can be with me.
Heart: When the time comes,
  you will climb down from that cross
  and leave me on it.
God: Is that what you want?
Heart: Part of me, yes.
God: And the other part?
Heart: God, I hate you.
God: Why are you crying?

Continue this dialogue with words of your own, or write a new one.

Chapter Five

An Experience of Spirit: Human Response

> *Some Israelites reviled Jesus one day as he was walking through their part of town.*
>
> *But he answered by repeating prayers in their name.*
>
> *Someone said to him:*
>
> *"You prayed for these men, did you not feel incensed against them?"*
>
> *He answered:*
>
> *"I could spend only of what I had in my purse."*[1]
>
> ATTAR OF NISHAPUR

*T*he experience of Spirit has been our concern all along. We uncovered its interpersonal origins in Jesus of Nazareth and its interpersonal continuance among the people of Spirit and Memory. All the creations of this people emerge from this foundational experience. To inhabit these creations with an open spirit is to be led, slowly but truthfully, into the labyrinthine relationship of God and the human person. We focused on a single creation—narrative, and explored the storytelling process. People tell their religiously significant experiences in story form and interpret them through the sacred story of Jesus; but they also hear the sacred story of Jesus and are urged to ponder and respond. In these two processes, the experience of Spirit gets under way. It is an experience that meets each person in his or her individuality; and so there are great surface differences. But if the story of Jesus is normative, there are some abiding concerns. The fullness of the experience of Spirit entails divine love, human sinfulness, the recreation of the person, and the reconciliation between people.

We have explored the encounter between divine love and human sinfulness. What must be looked at more extensively is the recreation of the person and the reconciliation between people. What will be the human response to the divine initiative? This story of Jesus and Peter gives us a start.

❧

"Goin' Fishin'"

It is known by everyone who cares to know that the Lord Jesus and Saint Peter used to retire to the local tavern after a hard day of ministry to break bread and drink wine together.

On a certain rainy night Saint Peter turned to the Lord Jesus and grinned. "We're doing real good."

"We?" asked the Lord Jesus.

Peter was silent. "All right, you're doing real good," he finally said.

"Me?" asked the Lord Jesus.

Peter pondered a second time. "All right, God's doing real good," he finally admitted.

But the Lord Jesus saw how reluctant Saint Peter was to

admit the source of all goodness. He laughed and hit the table with glee.

It was the laugh that got to Saint Peter. He pushed his face toward Jesus and blurted out, "Look! I was somebody before you came along. You didn't make me. I know now everybody says, 'There goes the Lord Jesus and his sidekick Saint Peter. Jesus cures them and Peter picks them up.' But it wasn't always that way. People knew me in my own right. I was respected and looked up to. They would say, 'There goes Peter, the greatest fisherman in all of Galilee.'"

"I heard that you were a very good fisherman, Peter," said the Lord Jesus, who was always ready to praise.

"You're damn right I was. And tomorrow I am going to prove it. We are going to go fishing and you will see how the other fishermen respect me and look to my lead."

"I would love to go fishing, Peter. I have never been fishing," said the Lord Jesus, who was always looking for new adventures. "But what will we do with all the fish we are going to catch?"

"Well," Peter smiled the smile of the fox. "We'll eat a few, store the rest, wait till there is a shortage, then put them on the market at top dollar and turn a big profit."

"Oh!" said the Lord Jesus, who had that puzzled and pained look in his face that Peter had often observed, as if something that had never crossed his mind just made a forced entry. Peter wondered how someone as obviously intelligent as Jesus could be so slow in some matters.

The next morning at dawn the Lord Jesus and Saint Peter were down at the shore readying their boat. And it was just as Saint Peter had said. When the other fishermen saw Peter, they sidled over. "Going out, Peter," they asked.

"Yeah," answered Peter, not looking up from the nets.

"Mind if we come along?"

"Why not?" shrugged Peter, pretending to be bothered by them.

When they left, he glared over at the Lord Jesus and said, "See!"

Saint Peter's boat led the way. The Lord Jesus was in the prow hanging on tightly for he was deeply afraid of the water. Now Saint Peter was a scientist of a fisherman. He tasted the water, scanned the sky, peered down into the lake—and gave the word in a whisper: "Over there."

"Why isn't anyone talking?" asked the Lord Jesus.

"Shhhh!" Peter shook his head.

The boats formed a wide circle around the area that Peter had pointed to. "Let down the nets," Peter's voice crept over the surface of the water.

"Why don't they just toss them in?" asked the Lord Jesus, who had hopes of learning about fishing.

A second shhhh! came from Saint Peter.

The fishermen let down their nets and began to pull them in. But something was wrong. The muscles of their arms did not tighten under the weight of fish. The nets rose quickly; the arms of the men were slack. All they caught was water.

The fishermen rowed their boats over to Saint Peter. They were a chorus of anger. "The greatest fisherman in all of Galilee, my grandmother's bald head. You brought us all the way out here for nothing. We have wasted the best hours of the day and have not one fish to show for it. Stick to preaching, Peter." And they rowed toward shore, shouting curses over their shoulder.

The Lord Jesus said nothing.

Saint Peter checked the nets. He put on a second parade, tasting the sea, scanning the sky, peering in to the depths. At long last he looked at the Lord Jesus and said, "Over there!"

No sooner had he said, "Over there!" than the Lord Jesus was at the oars, rowing mightily, the muscles of his back straining with each pull.

And all day long under the searing sun, the Lord Jesus and

Saint Peter rowed from place to place on the Sea of Galilee. And all day long under the searing sun, the Lord Jesus and Saint Peter let down their nets. And all day long under the searing sun, the Lord Jesus and Saint Peter hauled in their nets. And all day long under the searing sun, the Lord Jesus and Saint Peter caught nothing.

Evening fell and an exhausted Saint Peter raised the sail to make for shore. The weary Lord Jesus held on tightly in the prow.

It was then, as the boat glided toward shore, that it happened. All the fish in the Sea of Galilee came to the surface. They leapt on one side of the boat and they leapt on the other side of the boat. They leapt behind the boat and they leapt in front of the boat. They formed a cordon around the boat, escorting it toward shore in full fanfare.

Then in a mass suicide of fish, they began to leap into the boat. They landed in the lap of the laughing Lord Jesus. They smacked the astonished Saint Peter in the face. When the boat arrived at shore, it was brimming, creaking, sinking under the weight of fish.

All the other fishermen were waiting. They gathered around Peter and slapped him on the back. "Peter, you scoundrel. You knew where the fish were all the time and never let on." They hit him on the shoulder. "Peter, you rogue. You put us on. You surely are the greatest fisherman in all of Galilee."

But Saint Peter was uncharacteristically silent. He only said 'Give the fish to everyone. Tonight, no home in this village will go without food." After that, he said nothing.

But later at the tavern with bread and wine between them Peter looked across the table at Jesus and said, "Go away from me. You go away from me. I wanted the fish to be over them, not with them. I wanted the fish to rule them, not feed them. You go away from me. I am a sinful man.

But Jesus smiled, not the smile of the fox, but the smile

that swept over the waters at the dawn of time, the smile that moves the sun and the stars. And he had no intention of going away. There were other fish to catch.

❖❖❖

The story begins with Peter in the classic posture of the envious heart and ends with him in the initial posture of the forgiven heart. His opening line is a statement of self-justification "We're doing real good." Jesus' critical rejoinder, "We?" makes Peter think that Jesus, like the secret desire of his own heart, wants to take all the credit. Peter gives him the glory. But Jesus has no need to claim credit for the good that is happening. With the second response of "Me?" Peter realizes that Jesus is leading him into deeper waters of God. Peter reluctantly admits the source of all goodness; but Jesus catches the unconverted tone of this admission. With Jesus' laugh, Peter reverts to envy and asserts himself. "I am the greatest fisherman in all of Galilee" translates into "You, whoever you are, are not." Peter will now prove his importance at all costs.

The Lord Jesus is guileless. He is enthusiastic over the fishing expedition, tells Peter that he has heard of his fishing skills, and is an eager, if somewhat pesky, learner. He is also, like many Jews of his day, afraid of the water. Yet, vulnerable as he is, he is also the master and Peter will learn this day that God is a love that does not need his crowing and strutting. The fish have proved elusive; they are not available to the skills of the greatest fisherman in all of Galilee. The other fishermen abandon Peter in his failure. Jesus does not. He is the first to the oars to continue the search. It is the moment when both are exhausted, when all their efforts have been expended and found wanting that the gift of fish arrives.

The miracle of the suicidal fish leaping into the boat is the work of an ironic God, who abundantly gives us what we desperately want but not in the way we want it. Peter wants the fish as a conquering achievement, and they arrive as a comic gift. Through the mediation of Jesus, divine love is offering Peter a new possibility of being human. His initial responses to his personal event of grace show that he is tentatively moving toward accepting the gift. He does not bask in the emulation of the other fishermen. He knows that the old style is no longer appropriate. "Eat them. Store them. Make a killing." is replaced by "Give the fish to everyone. Tonight no home in this village will go without food." Whatever has happened, it has released other-centered energies in Peter. But at this moment Peter's giving away of the gift of fish is impulsive. It is neither understood nor integrated. The more brooding response occurs at the tavern. "Go away from me. I am a sinful man."

Love and Personal Response

The first response to the inrush of divine love is the recognition of sinfulness. We have grounded ourselves wrongly; and that wrong grounding has brought pain into the world. There will be no possibility of a new grounding and a new life unless the past is confessed. Christian conversion is not a movement from one stage of innocence to another. It is a movement from a struggle wrongly conceived to a struggle rightly conceived. We have become aware of our wrongly conceived struggle ("I am the greatest fisherman in all of Galilee") because the rightly conceived struggle initiated by divine love (How will we feed one another?) has infiltrated our consciousness. God has not done this for the purposes of condemnation, but for the purposes of transformation. But, as we intimated in the last chapter, the sudden exposure that we are sinners is extremely painful. It is not easy to say, "I wanted the fish to be over them, not with them." At this moment, we need a Love that loves us more than we love ourselves. That is why Jesus does not go away; but smiles the smile of creation for the new life of Peter is about to be born.

Personal re-creation entails surrender. William James has stated that "self-surrender has been and always must be regarded as the vital turning-point of the religious life."[2] E. D. Starbuck explores this moment insightfully.

> The act of yielding…is giving one's self over to the new life, making it the center of a new personality, and living, from within, the truth of it which had before been viewed objectively.[3]

The act of surrendering is really a process of recentering, a free acceptance of ourselves as constituted by a larger Power.

This recentering is a long and arduous process. The event of grace which reveals our sinfulness and offers the possibility of new life can usually be circumscribed quite neatly in time. "It happened when I was…" is a typical beginning when people relate conversion experiences.

But the response to these catalytic occurrences takes place over time. We only gradually see the implications of what has happened; and even more gradually find the personal courage and community support we need to change. We engage in the process of re-creation that we mapped out in chapter three. We tell and retell the experience; certain attitudes and outlooks become dominant; certain moral struggles begin to appear. Although the regrounding in God is a lifelong adventure, the general path of advance can be mapped. Surrender to divine love is the liberation of human love as revealed by the incident of the sinful woman at the house of Simon.

In this story, Jesus became angry. Gesturing at the sinful woman, he said to Simon, "Do you see this woman?" (Luke 7:44).

But Simon sees no woman. Simon sees a sinner, a theological category created by his own self-righteousness and maintained for his own importance. Simon is a portrait of self-enclosure. He thinks to himself that Jesus is not a prophet. A prophet is supposed to know the hearts of people and "if this man were a prophet, he would know who and what sort of woman this is who touches him—that she is a sinner."

But he does not venture to speak this opinion. He keeps it to himself, but that does not mean he keeps it away from Jesus. The man he does not think is a prophet knows Simon's inner thoughts. In response to Simon's thoughts, Jesus said to him, "Simon, I have something to propose to you." The cautious response is, "Teacher, speak." The story of the two debtors—one forgiven fifty coins and the other five hundred—ends with the simplest of questions. "Which of them was more grateful?" To the simplest of questions comes the most hesitant of responses, "He, I presume, to whom he remitted the larger sum." The "I presume" is the classic hedge of opportunism. Simon ventures nothing, neither his thoughts nor his values.

Jesus uncovers Simon's hidden heart by contrasting it with the heart of the woman. Simon has given Jesus no water for his feet; the woman has washed his feet with her tears and dried them with her hair. Simon has not given him a kiss of greeting; the woman has not ceased kissing his feet. Simon has not anointed his head with oil; the woman has anointed his feet with perfume.

The picture is complete. Simon is a miser. "He is like a person who holds on to the air inside his lungs, refusing to exhale it lest no more be available."[4] His whole life is one of "not giving." The woman, on the other hand, is total giving. She is pouring herself out on Christ. Her other-centered style is the polar opposite of the ego-centered style of Simon. Simon is a wary man in a wary world. She is a luxuriant woman in an extravagant world.

Jesus does not leave us in the dark about the source of

these two different ways of being alive. The most acceptable understanding of what Jesus says is that she is capable of loving because she has been forgiven; little love flows from those who have been forgiven little.[5] When divine love meets sin and the person recognizes her sinfulness and surrenders to the love, the result is the release of human love. The one who has found forgiving love, gives love. The one who has not found forgiving love, gives nothing. The empty heart of Simon only allows him to take; the full heart of the woman allows her to overflow. Simon stands back and judges; the woman embraces and cherishes.

Liberation From Egocentricity

A common characteristic of the envious and rejected heart is self-preoccupation. The rejected heart is obsessed with its insignificance; the envious heart is obsessed with its importance. But both are obsessed with themselves. Divine love is the release from this chronic egocentricity.

> Love is, therefore, on the one hand, the only salvation of the spiritual man and, on the other hand, unattainable by his own efforts. The spiritual man can only love when he is freed from the necessity of love, that is, when he knows himself already loved in his self-preoccupation. Only if man finds that he is already accepted in his sin and sickness can he accept his own self-preoccupation as it is; and only then can his psychic economy be opened toward others, to accept them as they are—not in order to save himself, but because he doesn't need to save himself. We love only because we are first loved. In this way, and only in this way, can the spiritual man genuinely and purely love.[6]

This dynamic underlies the woman's freedom. The experience of divine love becomes the possibility of human loving.

Divine love is not only the capacity for human love, but its inner energy. The concrete situation receives the emerging love of the forgiven person; but it does not control it. This is the thrust behind the story of Attar of Nishapur which opened this chapter. The ones who revile Jesus, he prays for. Their hostility cannot control his response.

Jesus can only give what is in his purse. He is coming from the experience of divine love and the resistances to embodying that love do not ultimately destroy it. The human love which divine love releases is free. This freedom is not indifference. Whenever love goes out, it is vulnerable. A person can be deeply hurt when his or her love is not received and returned. But when divine love is the force that suffuses human love, lack of response does not totally determine the flow of love. The sustained attitude of love is generated more by the experience of divine liberation than by the human reception.

The inner origins of Christian love are most clear in the command to love one's enemies. A situation of hostility would seem to dictate a hostile response. Yet the response suggested is the opposite of hatred—positive care. In the Gospel of Luke, enemy love is contrasted with situational love. "If you love those who love you, what credit is that to you?" (Luke 6:32).

If a receptive atmosphere is not the stimulation to love, what is the incentive? It is said that the nature of the divine is to be diffusive of itself. "It cannot not pour out." Whether the earth receives the water or not, the fountain continues to spring. When human love is released by divine love, it takes on this characteristic. It continues to move from inner abundance. It is co-loving all things with the ever outward love of God. When this energy of love is released, Teilard de Chardin suggested that the human race will have discovered fire for the second time.

Love of God, Love of Neighbor

But what does the person who has accepted divine love love? What are the "objects" of love? The compressed answer of the Gospels is the double commandment of love. "You shall love the Lord your God with all your heart, and with all your soul, and with all your strength, and with all your mind; and your neighbor as yourself" (Luke 10:27).

This double commandment suggests two directions—toward God and toward neighbor. From the sheer amount of words devoted to love of God, it would seem to have some priority. Yet the depth of Christian life is to envision these two directions as flowing from a single, responsive love. The continual task is to hold them together in a dynamic, mutual relationship, neither separating one from the other nor reducing one to the other. The reciprocity of love of God and love of neighbor is what we want to explore.

Responsive human love immediately moves toward the mediator of divine love. The outpouring of the forgiven heart is on the one who forgave it. The woman lavishes herself on Jesus, but not just on Jesus. She is loving Jesus as the bringer of forgiveness. Most commentaries on the story speculate that this is not her first encounter with Jesus. She has heard him preach; and the preaching reached her heart and stirred the Spirit of salvation. She has come in gratitude and praise to love the one who brought the Love. This is a natural movement of the redeemed heart. It loves the source of its redemption.

Although we have used a Scripture story to illustrate it, we do not have to resort to the Bible for examples of responsive gratitude. This is not an arcane truth; everyday life gives ample evidence of it. When someone brings us a love that liberates us, we respond with gratitude and commitment. We say, "I can't thank you enough."

We also feel a deep need to repay so unpayable a gift and we say, "If there is anything I can ever do for you...." Even time does not diminish our instinctive affective response to the love that loves us. Whenever we remember the people who have loved us and through their love redeemed us from destructiveness, our heart immediately goes out to them. From a religious perspective, we are first of all receivers of love; and the simple uncomplicated response is to love the love we have received.

We have stressed that divine and human love always come together; and although they can be distinguished, they can never be separated. But this ability to distinguish is important. In Jesus Christ, we have a full and perfect mediation of divine love. The mediated and the mediator have fused together so completely that to love one is to love the other.

The Gospel of John emphasizes this identity of Jesus and God. There is no instance in the Gospel where we are commanded to love God. But there is often the command, either implicitly or explicitly, to love the Son.[7] Jesus the Son has brought the love of the Father. Therefore to return love to the Son is to return love to the Father. All Christians are urged to love Christ, because through Christ they have encountered the plentitude of God's salvific love.

But besides Jesus Christ, there are the "other Christs" of the Christian tradition. These are the concrete persons who constitute the people of Spirit and Memory; and who, in their finest moments, have communicated divine love. They are usually parents, spouses, friends, and even, if the Gospel stories are to be credited, those we perceive as enemies.

Our response is to love them. But in them the fusion of the divine and the human is not what it was in Jesus. It is here that our need to distinguish comes into play. We recognize that their loving was co-loving. They were loving us with the love of God.

This does not diminish them or make them mere vehicles of grace. They are not dispensable channels of divine love, but cherished communicators. The divine moves through their uniqueness, ingenuity, and creativity. They are the human face of God. But this does not mean their own features are distorted. Their distinctiveness comes into its own beauty by being in union with divine beauty.

But human mediation, outside of Jesus, is flawed mediation. When we pretend this is not the case, we are ripe for disenchantment. We have turned the ones who have loved us into idols; and all idols have clay feet. The saints are the first to admit they are sinners. They know, as Francis of Assisi made explicit, they have become instruments of divine peace; but they also know at certain time and places they are instruments of human war. We can see the parent who loves us at one moment in a rage of spite and anger at another. The spouse who beheld our weakness and loved us anyway, now berates us in front of others. The friends who were there when we needed them are now nowhere to be found. Human loving is fragmented and partial. Yet in its mediating impact it reveals unconditional love. It is this divine love that remains, even if its human mediation fades.

Therefore, our responsive love encompasses the mediators, but goes beyond them. When this recognition occurs, we say "We love God." We perform a mental act of disengagement. We focus on the divine presence that comes through multiple created presences, but at this moment we are not consciously focusing on the created presences.

This is a natural procedure. A divine reality is perceived in the human reality. This divine love is truly other than the mediating human love.

Love and Prayer

A genuine option open to human perception is to focus on this divine love. Since it is this love that has cherished us, it is this love we wish to enter into a relationship with. Our response is to be attentive to it, engage it in dialogue, learn more about it. When liberated human love moves toward God, it begins to pray. "Thus praying is inseparable from love of God—it is the language of love which completes the relationship God initiates."[8]

The traditional analogy for prayer is a dialogue between two people who love each other; and this is a helpful way to explore the prayer life that arises from an encounter with divine love. In the first meeting, all the lovers know is the basic fact of their love. Their individual lives are "saved" when they are together and "lost" when they are apart.

With more encounters, there comes greater intimacy and a deepened appreciation of what their mutual love is accomplishing in them. There also develops a sense of responsibility to their love. They become aware of the conditions under which it will grow and the conditions under which it will atrophy. Prayer is the cultivation of the relationship which was consciously established in the experience of Spirit. Its purpose is to deepen, appreciate, and become more responsible to the reality of divine love.

This procedure of "segmenting out" the divine and pursuing a relationship with it may be natural; but it is also extremely dangerous. The danger lies in forgetting the roots of the relationship. The relationship came to be in a free, divine act of love which was mediated by other people. Any further communication within the relationship must not lose these qualities of divine initiative and relatedness to other people.

Yet the history of many people's prayer life reads like a chronicle of the solitary self's strenuous striving to gain the attention of a reluctant God. Prayer is not response to the reality of God that has chosen to engage us, but unaided assertion toward the reality of God that is constantly avoiding us. Prayer does not lead us into the depth of our encounters with other people, but provides an alternate reality for us to occupy ourselves with. In prayer we come to love a heavenly God while we are disdaining an earthly people. In order to understand the style of prayer that is appropriate to the experience of Spirit, we need to look at the prayer of the Giver of the Spirit.

The Prayer of Jesus

Before Jesus was an advocate of prayer, he was its most thoroughgoing critic.[9] He mocked the prayer of the righteous with its pompous boasting before God. "God, thank you that I am not like other people" (Luke 18:11). He brutally uncovered the real reason behind the public display of prayer—self-advertisement (Matthew 6:5). He outrageously linked outward piety with acts of injustice. "Beware...they devour widows' houses and for the sake of appearance say long prayers" (Mark 12:40).

Jesus attacked the core assumption of all professional prayers that more is better. "When you are praying, do not heap up empty phrases as the Gentiles do; for they think that they will be heard because of their many words" (Matthew 6:7–8). Finally, and most scathingly, he took up the ancient prophetic denunciation of substituting prayer for just action. "Not everyone who says to me, 'Lord, Lord,' will enter the kingdom of heaven, but only the one who does the will of my Father in heaven" (Matthew 7:21). In the light of this consistent critique, it is not an idle question when one of his disciples asks, "Lord, teach us to pray" (Luke 11:1).

The reason that Jesus so vigorously attacked the prayer practices of his day is that they contradicted the Abba-King experience of God. The prayer practices show frightened and panicky people before an all-powerful presence they cannot be sure of. These people alternately boast and babble, doing anything to get the attention of a God who is basically bored with them. Their prayer is just one more strategy in the overall campaign of ego glorification. To pray in public for attention and rip off widows in private for security is perfectly compatible. Both flow from the shaken self, desperately grasping for something to hold on to. In short, these prayers are not a response to the inrush of divine love, but a sign of the stubborn resistance to accept our lives as given from beyond ourselves.

Prayer that is a loving response to divine love takes many different forms. But there is a definite "coloration" to the activity. There is an atmosphere to the relationship, a feeling-tone that permeates all the interactions. Whatever the particular content of prayer might be, these qualities are present and influential. We will try to point out three characteristics of this type of prayer. Our guide will be Jesus' classic prayer, the Our Father.

First, the divine and the human are held together and the bonds between people strengthened. The first line of the Lord's prayer is "Our Father in heaven." Although prayer may be said in solitude, it always addresses the reality that binds people together. The opening word must be "our." If it is not, we are in danger of creating a private God, one who looks after us but is neglectful of others. Prayer would then foster division, because some would have the ear of God and some would not. But the God encountered in Christian prayer is the grounding of human solidarity. The divine love that is dialogued with talks to more than me; and so through it, I am related to all others. As the poet Anne Sexton put it: "To pray, Jesus knew, / is to be a man carrying a man."

Although the Father is characterized as in heaven and so transcendent to the affairs of earth, the very fact that we can say "Father" indicates divine presence. The portrait is definitely different than the Oriental Potentate God who lives in the sky and can only be contacted through the bribes of slaughtered cattle and burnt wheat.

The God of Jesus' prayer has already made contact, and his contact has brought life. So he is called "Father." The life that has been given comes from beyond ourselves, from an Otherness that is the source of all created reality. So we say "in heaven." But the perception is clear. The divine and the human are not alienated, but in intimate communion.

This interaction of the divine and the human is considerably deepened in the "forgiveness" section of the Lord's Prayer. This petition seems to say that the proper response to the experience of divine love is to transform it into human love toward one another. The energy and inspiration of this human love will be perceived as divine: "Let your light shine before others, so that they may see your good works and give glory to your Father in heaven" (Matthew 5:16).

If we have been forgiven, we are to forgive in turn. When we do this, we do more than merely "give as we have received." In the fact of loving others, we enter more deeply into our own experience of divine love. As Norman Perrin puts it: "In the context of God's forgiveness men learn to forgive, and in the exercise of forgiveness toward their fellow man they enter ever more deeply into an experience of the divine forgiveness."[10]

The atmosphere of the prayer "which passionately pursues the divine love that has passionately pursued the person" is the intimate bonding of God, self, and neighbor.

A second quality of the prayer that cultivates divine love is that it is other-centered and strategic. After the initial address in the Lord's Prayer, the priorities are set out. "Your name be held holy; your kingdom come; your will be done, on earth as in heaven." The concerns are not those of the one praying; they are those of the one prayed to.

These petitions purify the desires of the person before God. The one praying has experienced love and expressed it as "Our Father." The response to this love is to espouse the concerns of the Lover. This is the true maturity of prayer. Prayer is not pleading with an unfeeling Higher Power to do our bidding. It is not a begging of God to do for us what we cannot do for ourselves. This procedure, all too common in prayer, subtly places us at the center of the universe and reverses the creature-creator relationship. Prayer is for the purpose of discerning the cause of God in human life and marshaling our energies to serve it.

In prayer, we lay ourselves open to the cause of God. Nikos Kazantzakis opens his autobiography, *Report to Greco,* with three prayers. "Three kinds of souls, three prayers: (1) I am a bow in your hands, Lord, draw me, lest I rot; (2) Do not over-draw me, Lord. I shall break; (3) Overdraw me, Lord, and who cares if I break."[11] In prayer we become available for the divine mission. We must be careful of this. It easily turns to fanaticism. The only check is the reminder that the divine cause is love.

Prayer then is for plotting. In the overall story of Jesus, the rhythm of prayer and action is firmly established. Jesus prays at times of important decisions—when he chooses the twelve, when he sets his face toward Jerusalem, when the influential and powerful decide against him, when he faces the possibilities of suffering, when death finally comes. In the middle of a whirlwind ministry and in the face of growing opposition, Jesus retires to desert places to pray. The implication is that the path of love is not all that easily discerned.

And if prayer does not complement action, action will go its own way, breaking loose from divine love and inevitably betraying it. Nowhere is this more evident than in the Gethsemane prayer: "Abba, Father, for you all things are possible; remove this cup from me; yet, not what I want, but what you want" (Mark 14:36). In prayer we gauge our situation and project the path that will most serve God's cause.

This fact that prayer is other-centered and strategic means that it can never be divorced from experience and action. On the one hand, prayer flows out of the experience of divine love we have undergone. It is meditation on the implications of that experience and the cultivation of the relationship which was established at that time.

On the other hand, prayer looks to the further embodiment of that experience. It envisions actions that will be congruent with it. Any type of prayer that does not stem from experience or has no overflow into action is too isolated. Prayer may provide times of ecstasy; but as long as that ecstasy is experienced by people in the throes of sin and grace, it cannot be an end itself. The touch of God always means personal and social transformation.

The third constant quality of praying out of the experience of divine love has to do with the affective flow of the relationship. Divine love initiated the relationship, but mutual love sustains it. Prayer is a conversation between hearts. It includes the traditional praise and gratitude, an occasional scream for help, a fervent petition now and then, and some hard-nosed bargaining for a better deal.

But it does not stop there. It encompasses the confiding of secrets, the admission of fears, the free flow of tears, and ecstatic dance. When you start a conversation with "Abba," anything is liable to happen. Divine love is abundance; and in relationship to it, abundant feelings and insights emerge. And if you are steeped in the anthropomorphism of the Bible, God is an avid conversationalist.

Prayer that is more than duty includes religious affections. It is a nurturing activity that provides "bread for the day." The qualities of trust, intimacy, warmth, delight, and exuberance are often present. But this God is not a chum or a mere fellow traveler. The transcendence of God always remains. This is the God whose ways are not our ways and whose uncovered face spells death. Yet the majesty of the divine does not mean coldness. Can there be such a thing as friendly transcendence and warm majesty? The poets think so.

> I'm mooring my rowboat
> at the dock of the island called God
> This dock is made in the shape of a fish
> and there are many boats moored
> at many different docks.
> "It's okay," I say to myself,
> with blisters that broke and healed
> and broke and healed—
> saving themselves over and over.
> And salt sticking to my face and arms like
> a glue-skin pocked with grains of tapioca.
> I empty myself from my wooden boat
> and onto the flesh of The Island.
> "On with it." He says and thus
> we squat on the rocks by the sea
> and play—can it be—
> a game of poker.
> He calls me.
> I win because I hold a royal straight flush.
> He wins because He holds five aces.
> A wild card had been announced
> but I had not heard it
> being in such a state of awe
> when He took out the cards and dealt.
> As he plunks down His five aces
> and I sit grinning at my royal flush,
> He starts to laugh,

the laughter rolling like a hoop out of His mouth
and into mine,
and such laughter that He doubles right over me
laughing a Rejoice Chorus at our two triumphs.
Then I laugh, the fishy dock laughs
the sea laughs. The Island laughs.
The Absurd laughs.
Dearest dealer,
I, with my royal straight flush,
love you so for your wild card,
that untamable, eternal, gut-driven *ha-ha*
and lucky love.[12]

Christian life is living in relationship to a transcendent, loving reality. It is beyond our control yet not oblivious of the desires of our heart. It calls wild cards with little or no notice; and, although we are outraged, we love it all the more for that. Within the Christian tradition, we believe the final wild card is resurrection.

To be touched by divine love through other people is to love the divine back through those same people. But we are capable of focusing on the divine more directly; and we do this in prayer. But this prayer does not leave behind the earth; it pushes us more deeply into the heart of the world. We focus on God as the source of human solidarity, the power that transforms personal and social life, and the loving reality that sustains us, but does not submit to us.

It is this last quality that we must explore further. What does it mean for people to love a divine reality which, however immanent and understandable, remains transcendent and unknowable. This is the struggle that the gospels of Matthew, Mark, and Luke portray the moment Jesus leaves the waters of sin with the word *Son* in his ears.

The Temptations of Jesus

No sooner is Jesus baptized than he is "led by the Spirit in the wilderness, where for forty days he was tempted by the devil" (Luke 4:1–2). The temptations of Jesus in the desert are often understood as possible false uses of messianic power. Jesus has been declared the beloved Son at the baptism; and that sonship entails a mission. The question is how he will carry out his assignment; what will be his strategies.

Satan has some suggestions. He should use his power to provide a kingdom of bread which will feed all people. Jesus responds that there is more to life than bread. Satan's second proposal is that Jesus float down from the pinnacle of the Temple. This will establish his authority beyond doubt; and people will eagerly follow him from miracle to miracle.

When this strategy is rejected, Satan suggests they join forces for world domination. Political conquest is the way the mission should be enacted. Dostoyevsky's Grand Inquisitor is the classic proponent of this interpretation. He tells the silent Jesus that if he really loved people he would have fed them, relieved their doubts with miracles, and imposed global government. Instead he left them their freedom, a dubious gift at best.

This approach to the temptations has far-reaching implications and has been effectively used in understanding the social and political dimensions of Christian faith. But another approach sees the three temptations as christological rather than soteriological.[13] It is not Jesus' relationship to other people that is being tested, but his relationship to God.

The title under which Satan tempts him is not "Messiah," but "Son of God." Also, the fact that the Spirit led him into the wilderness recalls Israel's sojourn in the desert of sin after the Exodus liberation. That story concerns the rocky relationship between Yahweh and his people. In the desert, Israel was tested and found wanting. The apologetic interests of the early

Church place Jesus in the same desert. He will be tested and found to be the true Son. In the context of our concerns, the temptations tell us more about what it means to return love to God.

Significant portions of the Bible portray the relationship between Yahweh and his people as a stormy love affair. What makes for the storm is that at various times both partners feel unappreciated and misunderstood. The declared love between them is not being lived out the way they had expected. They look for new pledges of love that are both spoken and enacted. In chapter four, we traced the insidious way the sinful heart put God to the test in search of a pledge of love. The result is succinctly stated in Romans: "But God proves his love for us in that while we still were sinners Christ died for us" (Romans 5:8).

This divine sharing in the human condition revitalizes the love relationship: "For I am convinced that neither death, nor life, nor angels, nor rulers, nor things present, nor things to come, nor powers, nor height, nor depth, nor anything else in all creation, will be able to separate us from the love of God in Christ Jesus our Lord" (Romans 8:38).

Looking at the cross of Christ the human heart can say, "Now I know."

But sin not only tests God before people. In our reformulated understanding of testing narratives, it also tests people before God. The temptations of Jesus represent the trials love for God will undergo. They are episodes that detail Jesus' steadfast love, love that endures all the doubts and terrors that beset it.

The traditional Christian statement of faith in Christ is that he is truly God and truly man. When we were exploring divine love for people, we stressed the divine dimension of Jesus Christ and his life as revelatory of God's intentions. The death of the Son of God is the assurance of divine love.

We are now exploring how people love God; so we will stress the human dimension and his life as revelatory of a full human response. Christ is "not only the offer of divine love to man made visible but, at the same time, as prototype (or primordial model), he is the supreme realization of the response of human love to this divine offer."[14]

The First Temptation

The first temptation takes place in the desert and so recalls Israel's testing in the desert of sin (Exodus 16, 17). Yahweh had led Israel out of Egypt. In Yahweh's eyes, they should love him for this act alone. But in the desert they begin to grumble. "If only we had died at the hand of the LORD in the land of Egypt, when we sat by our fleshpots and ate our fill of bread; for you have brought us out into this wilderness to kill this whole assembly with hunger" (Exodus 16:3).

So Yahweh hears their grumbling and gives them manna in the morning and quail at evening. But already there is the beginning of a problem. As later rabbis commented, Yahweh gave the manna with a light countenance, but the quail with a heavy countenance. Yahweh's command that comes with this gift of food is that they may not gather the manna on the Sabbath. Some break this command, but they find no manna on the ground. The countenance of Yahweh grows darker.

Then at Massah the grumbling grows louder. "Give us water to drink." They demand another miracle and make it the condition for knowing "Is the Lord in our midst or not?" Yahweh hears them again and tells Moses, "Strike the rock, and the water will flow from it for the people to drink." But there is little doubt that the character of Yahweh in the story whose feelings are reflected in Moses is beginning to wonder if the people he loves love him in return.

The trouble between Yahweh and his people is often stated

as lack of trust. The Israelites doubted whether God would take care of them. But this is only the surface of the difficulty. Yahweh has given them freedom from slavery. But they want more. Every time any need arises they petition God to fill it. And Yahweh, in his love for them, does fill it. Bread, meat, and water miraculously arrive.

But it is beginning to dawn on Yahweh that his love may be one-sided. They are taking Yahweh for granted and turning him into a "go-for." From God's point of view he is being taken advantage of. He is not loved, but only used for what he can provide; and the moment he stops providing, their praise turns to grumbling. No crisis is integrated into the past loving history of the relationship. Each crisis threatens the relationship itself. This is a sure sign that God is not loved, but only manipulated for his gifts. After each gift is greedily accepted, the people respond, "Thank you. But what have you done for us lately?"

This is the atmosphere of the first go-around between Jesus and Satan. Jesus is hungry and Satan suggests that a divine miracle is the ideal way to fulfill that need. "If you are the Son of God, command these stones to turn into bread." Jesus replies, "Not on bread alone is man to live, but on every word that comes from the mouth of God."

At the baptism, a word has already come from the mouth of God; and the word was "Beloved Son." There is no need to test that word at every turn. Satan is playing upon the possibility in Jesus of a petulant and greedy heart. "If you really love me, then.... " He does not want any stability in the relationship between Jesus and God. He wants each new happening to be "the be-all and end-all" of the relationship. When the people of Israel hungered, they forgot that Yahweh rescued them from Egypt. Satan wants Jesus' hunger to so dominate him that he will forget the loving word of the water and demand a new miracle—not a voice from the sky, but bread from stone. And, oh yes, what Satan leaves unsaid, tomorrow there will be a need for another miracle.

This temptation strikes at the heart of all faith. There is no problem in loving God when the sun shines. It is the rain that brings doubt. In the Book of Job, Satan chides God with the remark, "Is it for nothing that Job is God-fearing?" And he recounts Job's many blessings. His smug observation is that if you take away the blessings, Job's love of God will soon turn to cursing.

What is fascinating in this temptation is the idealism of the human lover and the realism of the divine lover. From the human point of view, pain, suffering, and death should not happen and are taken as signs of an indifferent God. From the divine point of view, pain, suffering, and death are going to happen, why take them as signs of the lack of love? The key to God's point of view in the narratives is that he has declared his love "no matter what." The foundation of human trust in God in times of want and crisis are the previous experiences of divine fidelity.

An illuminating approach to this Satan-Jesus dialogue is to see Satan as concentrating on satisfaction-assurance and Jesus as countering with reality-assurance. These terms are coined by Donald Evans.[15] Satisfaction-assurance means that all our physical and emotional needs are being met. Reality-assurance is the assurance that life is worth living, because it has already "received the meaning and the reality which are necessary for human fulfillment."[16] These twin assurances are related yet distinct. When there is food, clothing, friendship, and shelter to satisfy us, we are to take these "goods" as symbols of an ultimate assurance. But when these are lacking, we do not take the lack as symbols of an ultimate rejection. In these situations, we fall back on our deeper sense of reality-assurance. This is what Jesus does. He will not take the lack of bread as a symbol of his lack of worth, the fact that God does not love him. His worth has already been established. He will integrate his hunger into the word of the water—"Beloved Son."

The Second Temptation

The second temptation takes place on the parapet of the Temple. The Temple is the place of special divine protection; and this temptation has to do with twisting divine love into special privilege. Satan proposes that Jesus' sonship is a prerogative to be exploited. The proper response to divine love is to parade the fact that you are loved. Jesus' insistence is that you do not love the fact that you are loved, but you love the Love that loves you.

This means that you will pursue that Love even when your own life is slipping away. In the Gospel of Luke, the temptation narrative ends with "the devil left him…to await another opportunity." Satan's finest opportunity is when life is ebbing in Jesus. On the cross, Satan waits to see if Jesus can love God and God's work when God is not shielding him.

The words of Jesus on the cross in Luke are "Father, forgive them for they know not what they do." Jesus is the Son; and that does not mean protection from harm but concern, above all, with salvific presence of God. Loving God is just that—loving God. It is not loving the fact that you are loved.

James Mackey has an insightful passage about what loving God in the face of death means.

> Like the rest of us, the man Jesus came from nothing and he had nothing except what was given to him. His very life and everything which came to him in life was gift. Out of the bounty freely given he freely gave. Life itself, and everything that became part of that life, he held as a grace, as one holds a precious gift, gently, as one holds a soft, delicate thread which, as it is drawn

back will, if one does not pull at it and break it, draw one to its very source. With this lived conviction, this faith that is made real only in act, he inspired some, and as deeply offended the deepest convictions of others. When force was brought to bear on him, inevitably, in order to make him divide and grasp like the rest, then, in final witness to the faith by which he lived and by which alone life is served, he refused to do so. He held the thread as gently as ever, as it was drawn back, and in doing so he deprived death of its sting, robbed it of its only victory. Death's victory over us is to enslave us in fear, to make us grasp more eagerly and tear more savagely at the things we think can give us the life we want, and, as we do so, feel more utterly the futility, and fear more persistently the hopelessness of it all. Jesus denied death that victory.

In denying death that victory, Jesus recorded the only victory over death, but also the one real victory over death, which is given to mortals to achieve. The Prince of Life was victorious over death in the act of dying. The one whose conviction of grace had wagered for life in life, whose living faith had overcome in life the agents of death, the grasping, tearing divisions of humankind, now consummated the victory of life over death by still treating life as grace at the one moment in which the conviction that life is gift is subjected to the ultimate test, the final trial, the moment when the gift is withdrawn. His death was the supreme act of faith in God the Father, the giver of the grace of life, and so it was the supreme act of hope.[17]

Loving God is not exemption from harm, but the faithful pursuit of love in the face of death.

Loving God is a difficult idea for many to appreciate today. It seems so abstract, especially when it is compared to
loving the person next to you. But loving God means valuing
Love more than life and death. It means appreciating the ultimate worthwhileness of life without needing to survive, and
usually to survive in style, at every moment. Most statements
about loving God in our culture are indirect homages. One of
the finest comes from Henri Nouwen. He is reflecting on his
fiftieth birthday.

> Within a few years (five, ten, twenty, or thirty) I will
> no longer be on this earth. The thought of this does
> not frighten me but fills me with a quiet peace. I am a
> small part of life, a human being in the midst of thou-
> sands of other human beings. It is good to be young, to
> grow old, and to die. It is good to live with others, and
> to die with others. God became flesh to share with us
> in this simple living and dying and thus made it good.
> I can feel today that it is good to be and especially to
> be one of many. What counts are not the special and
> unique accomplishments in life that make me different
> from others, but the basic experiences of sadness and
> joy, pain, and healing, which make me part of human-
> ity. The time is indeed growing short for me, but that
> knowledge sets me free to prevent mourning from de-
> pressing me and joy from exciting me. Mourning and
> joy can now both deepen my quiet desire for the day
> when I realize that the many kisses and embraces I re-
> ceived today were simple incarnations of the eternal
> embrace of the Lord himself.[18]

What is interesting in reading this beautiful yet indirect passage on the love of God is that our minds immediately move to
"refuting situations." This felt-perception may be possible at

the birthday party, but what about a deathbed or worse, a torture chamber. We always envision a test case to see if this "state of soul" is permanent or only an illusory peace. We may be a long way from the cultural testing patterns of ancient Israel; but there is still an instinct that says the truth is only known in fire.

The Third Temptation

The third temptation in the Gospel of Matthew is for Jesus to change allegiance. Satan takes him to a mountaintop where he can see the kingdoms of the world and offers him everything if only he will bow down and worship him. This temptation is properly placed. Jesus has just opted for an invisible Love. He has stated that he will love God when the mediations of love are lacking (the bread) and when he is not protected from the powers of diminishment and death.

This appears to be a groundless love. Satan is offering him something concrete. He seems to be saying, "You love a God who won't prove it. Love me, and I'll prove it. Take the earth over this heaven you are guessing at." Jesus' response seems to be "I cannot love you because you are not Love." The ultimate truth of Jesus' response to his experience of God as Abba is that he cannot love anything that does not manifest Love.

This is the most telling reason why love of God cannot be collapsed into love of neighbor. The brutal fact is that the neighbor will not be loved authentically unless God is co-loved in the act of loving the neighbor. Unless there is a vision of sustaining and transforming love and a commitment to it above all else, it is too easy to give in.

Satan is right. The long haul of trying to love in the absence of mediations and protection moves inevitably to the strategy of quick, short gains at the expense of others. "No one can serve two masters," said Jesus. But a person can move back and forth, serving God when convenient and serving mammon when convenient. It is often stressed that Christian faith does not hold that Jesus was not tempted. It holds that he did not sin. There are many renditions of what this means. Perhaps it is just simply that he could not bring himself to love what was not Love.

Our core conviction is that the surrender to divine love means the liberation of human love. This liberated love moves in two complementary directions, toward God and toward neighbor. In the movement toward God, human love encompasses the mediators and goes through them to the permeating divine love. It cultivates this divine love in prayer.

This prayer relationship is a mapping of the ways of divine love as it binds people together and solicits human cooperation in its sustaining and transforming activity. But it also situates the one who prays in a living relationship to a transcendent graciousness. This means, among other things, living in a Love we cannot control and whose ways remain a mystery to us.

Anything beyond our control and which is not constantly solicitous of us on our own terms we tend to dismiss. The temptations of Jesus spell out the inevitable problems. We must love the Love that loves us even when mediation and protection are missing and the desire to grasp and tear and divide and conquer are overwhelming. It is with this divine love in our hearts that we co-love our neighbor as the following story illustrates.

⋅⋟⋞⋅

The Baker

The front of the unemployment office is all brick. The street never sees what happens inside. Next to this building is a bakery with a plate-glass window. Every day everybody who passes can see the baker "doing whatever it is that bakers do." Lately the baker has taken to doing "unbakerlike" things. He is making sandwiches at lunch time and giving them to people waiting in the unemployment lines. He will not take any money.

This is news. So the television mini-cam people arrived to get the scoop. They interviewed the baker who stood outside his shop like a giant jelly roll.

"Why are you doing this?"

"When I was twenty, I went hungry for a week. Finally, a man I'll never forget took me in." The baker stopped. He said no more. He just smiled as if everything was now accounted for.

⋅⃰⃰⃰⃰

Whatever happened to the baker when he was twenty, from a Christian point of view he got the message. He not only remembers and loves the one who fed him, he feeds others. The response to love received is love passed on. We would need more conversation to see if in the human love he received he discerned a larger love; and if in his care for others, he was communicating to them a larger care. But, as is usually the case in contemporary life, divine love is incognito. It is intuited and relied on but seldom made explicit.

In Christian code, the baker probably did not see Christ in the man who fed him; and he probably does not see Christ in the hungry he feeds. There is no doubt the judgment of Christ will provoke surprise in most people, "When did I see you hungry..." (Matthew 25). But also this passage seems to suggest that explicitation is secondary. What is important is to be there when being there is what is needed.

But we are trying to make connections, to uncover the depth of love received and loved passed on. Our not-so-modest suggestion (which would have to be checked out) is that the baker loved the man who fed him in God and is loving the ones he feeds in God. If he did not love God through his love for the one who fed him, he would not be in the lunch business. He would remember the person who fed him as an example of kindness and himself as one "lucky son-of-a-bitch" to have bumped into him when he did. But there would be no impulse to feed others.

The reason the baker feeds others is because, as the second half of the double commandment says, he sees them as himself. The underlying power that allows us to see the other as ourselves is the power that connects the two of us—the power of God. To love God is to experience a baffling solidarity with other people.

Christians have construed this relationship between the love of God and the love of neighbor in many different ways. One of the most destructive renditions of the relationship is to see them as competing interests. When the question is phrased, "Who do you love more, God or your neighbor?" we are already on the wrong track.

But this is a track many have taken. Total love of God demands the loss of earth. If you love God, you forsake the world; and if your love of "worldly things" is too great, God is certainly not being adequately attended to. The most cited scriptural backing for this tension is in Matthew: "Whoever loves father or mother more than me is not worthy of me, and whoever loves son or daughter more than me is not worthy of me" (Matthew 10:37).

This is a jealous God and a jealous Christ who wants the undivided attention of their worshipers. Love of God is not the transformation of love for others, but its substitute.

People who hold strongly to this heavy contrast position can find themselves in a somewhat ludicrous and illogical problem. They say they love God more than anything else. In fact, their intense love of God has made them indifferent to the concerns of earth. This life and its loves are passing. Set your heart on eternal treasure.

But the God they love loves the concerns of earth. The entire Christian revelation revolves around God's unrelenting activity in time and history. Loving God certainly means loving what God loves. This is the polemical edge of the First Letter of John. "Those who say, 'I love God,' and hate their brothers or sisters, are liars; for those who do not love a brother or sister whom they have seen, cannot love God whom they have not seen" (4:20–21). The competition scheme not only leads to odious comparisons; it also subtly suggests an essential rift between God and his creation.

A second misunderstanding deals with the motivation for loving the neighbor. The logic runs this way: We are children of God who love what God loves. God loves everybody; his love is universal. Therefore, we love everybody because God does. This syllogistic procedure has its problems. First, the neighbor in his or her uniqueness is lost. Our universalist motivation obscures the particularity of the person loved. We love them for an outside reason, a reason external to their individuality. The one who is loved says inside herself or himself: "This person loves me because God loves me, not because of anything I am in myself." But what we all want is a love that embraces us in all our irreducible otherness. W. H. Auden spelled it out, "For the error bred in the bone / Of each woman and man / Craves what it cannot have / Not universal love / But to be loved alone."[19]

Loving from a divine universalist motivation overlooks the warts; and everybody knows there can be no real love that misses the warts.

Second, external divine motivation often plays into a faulty understanding of how God loves. In Mary Gordon's *Final Payments* Isabel More reflects: "I would love Margaret now as God loved his creatures: impartially, impervious to their individual natures and thus incapable of being really hurt by them....I could not love with God's intensity. But I would choose His mode: the impartial, the invulnerable, removed from loss."[20]

This understanding distances the lover from the one loved. There is very little compassionate sharing of the life of the one loved. What there is is risk-free help. There is aid from the outside, but no involvement from the inside. To say this is how divine love works is an effective denial of the incarnation. To parody this style of loving in the human world is to become the saddest of all sights, the joyless giver.

This motivation scheme has an even more externalist rendition. It is not that God loves the neighbor and so then do we; but that God has commanded it and we must obey. The interconnection of love of God and neighbor begins and ends on the level of obligation. No deeper understanding is sought.

The argument is airtight. Love of neighbor does not entail affectionate feelings. If that were the case, the category of neighbor would be constricted to friends. Loving is not liking. Why, then, do we love our neighbor? God has commanded love of neighbor and attached rewards and punishments to the command. Loving the neighbor is not a matter of the heart, but a matter of the will; and the will is under the sovereign dictates of God, what Kierkegaard called "the shalt of eternity."

If the command is obeyed, the reward is heaven; if it is disobeyed, the punishment is hell. Therefore, if you love God and hear his commands, love your neighbor. This understanding turns the neighbor into a steppingstone. Heaven is the goal; helping people I do not like is the means.

Love of God is neither in competition with love of neighbor nor is it the external motivation for loving others. How should the bonding between them be understood. Gunther Bornkamm starts us in the right direction.

> Surrender to God now no longer means a retreat of the
> soul into a paradise of spirituality and the dissolution
> of selfhood in adoration and mediation, but a waiting
> and preparedness for the call of God, who calls to us in
> the person of our neighbor. In this sense the love our
> neighbor is the test of our love of God.[21]

Loving God makes us attentive to dimensions of reality which
we might otherwise overlook. We see and hear differently.[22]
The rejected heart saw all things devalued. The envious heart
saw all things in competition. The forgiven heart sees all things
immersed in the love of God.

Loving God enables the neighbor to be seen. At the most
radical level, the problem is that the neighbor is invisible. We
have explored the parable of the Good Samaritan twice, in
chapter two and chapter four. A third foray into this remarkable story will prove helpful. In the tale, three people notice
the man in the ditch. The priest and the Levite look at him and
pass by. The Samaritan sees him and is moved with compassion. But do they all see the same reality?

This story is set within the framework of the double commandment. In particular, it explores the second commandment,
"Love your neighbor as yourself" because it is an answer to
the question, "Who is my neighbor?" In this context what
the priest and Levite see is "not me." What the Samaritan sees
is "me." He is moved with compassion because he is in the
ditch.

There are many interpretations of loving your neighbor as
yourself. One is the golden rule: do unto others as you would
want them to do unto you. This takes our natural self-love
and extends it into a universal principle. Kierkegaard has
insightfully spelled out this dynamic.

If we are to love our neighbor AS OURSELVES, then this commandment opens, as with a master-key, the lock of our self-love and snatches it away from us. Should the commandment to love our neighbor be formulated in another way than by the expression AS THYSELF, which can be handled so easily and yet has the tension of all eternity, the commandment could not master our self-love so effectively. The meaning of AS THYSELF cannot be twisted and turned; judging man with the insight of eternity, it penetrates the innermost part of his soul, where his egoism resides. It does not allow our egoism to make the least excuse, nor to evade it in any way. What a wonderful thing! One might have made longer penetration speeches about the way man should love his neighbor, but again and again our egoism would have managed to produce excuses and evasions, because the matter would not have been completely exhausted, a certain aspect would have passed over, a point would not have been described precisely enough or would not have been sufficiently binding in its expression. This AS THYSELF however—truly, no wrestler could clasp his opponent more firmly or inextricably than this commandment clasps our egoism.[23]

As clever and persuasive as this rendition is, there is not-so-subtle glorification of egoism. The one loving is not freed from self-preoccupation but trapped within it, and then forced by an internal logic to move outside the person. More importantly, there is no overt connection with loving God. There is no indication that the self this person is seeing in the neighbor is the self that is loved by God and loves God in return.

How do people who have experienced God's love for them and love God in return love themselves? They love themselves as loved by God. If they had cultivated a rejected heart, they secretly hated themselves. They were nobodies, uncared for by the origin and destiny of their lives. They acted out their insignificance by becoming socially insignificant.

If they cultivated an envious heart, they secretly questioned their lovability. They bolstered it every chance they had because they were so unsure of it. They acted out this inner panic by acquiring for themselves the "things" that would make them valuable and depriving others of those same "things."

The only way that these two hearts could love themselves was if someone loved them, independent of their self-depreciation in the first case and their self-aggrandizement in the second case. They both had to come to the awareness that they were the unique recipient of a free, unconditional love.

This is the self the Samaritan sees in the ditch. He loves him as he loves himself, as the unique recipient of divine love. He is not a rich man or a poor man, or a Jew or a Gentile, or a man or a woman, or a master or a slave. All these are categories which may be needed for the well-ordering of society; but they have been superseded by divine love. Co-loving the neighbor with the love of God means uncovering their uniqueness and responding to them as an actual other. The forgiven heart is a perceptive heart.

> The more deeply we penetrate into a man through an understanding cognition guided by personal love, the more unsubstitutable, irreplaceable, nonexchangeable, individual, and unique does he become for us. So much the more do the various "wrappings" that are there fall from his individual personal center. These "wrappings" refer to the more or less social "self" of the man, the general bondage to similar drives, needs of life, and passion, as well as to the idols of language that hide from us the individual nuances of experience insofar as they allow us to apply the same words and signs to them.[24]

The love of God in our heart has opened our eyes to the unique worth of each person.

It is each person too. A consistent comment on the parable of the Good Samaritan is that the categories of neighbor and enemy are abolished. The neighbor is simply the next person met, especially if he or she is in need. Kierkegaard summed it up succinctly: "If there are only two men, the other man is the neighbor; if there are millions, each one of these is the neighbor."[25]

The terrible effect of seeing all people in God is that our enemies are taken from us. Enemies supply energy. When we wake each morning in mode of anger and attack, we know we are alive. We may lose the battles we are mentally envisioning, but the task is clear: dragons abound, dragon slayer.

But when the enemy becomes the sinner, a strange perceptual shift occurs. The enemy's aggression flows from his or her shaken center and reflects a frantic flight from God. When we see this in the enemy, we know all about it. We have been there. It is different each time we see it; but it is similar enough for the message to get through. The enemy is "ourselves"; and we must love this enemy in his or her sin as we were loved in our sin. This is not mental gymnastics or psychological reductionism. It is simply what the heart that loves God sees.

What we see is what we love. The love of God sees each person embracing and resisting divine and human love. The person who co-loves her neighbor with the love of God inserts herself into this dynamic. This love does not confer value on the person from outside. It spies the real value which is struggling to emerge. Love is not blind, but a process of penetrating sight. It knows the heart and helps it toward salvation.

> Persons who hate themselves often come to discover and love their ideal essence through responsive co-loving with the one who loves them. Zacchaeus came to love

what Jesus loved in him. When we love, we make it possible for the beloved to be transformed and ultimately to achieve that salvation which is the destiny toward which God's creative love is beckoning. The Christian God is not merely a Grecian all-knowing God who contemplates eternal essences in himself; he is an all-loving God who redeems his creation. When we co-love with God's love, we effectively co-create with God the beloved's salvation.[26]

Co-creating with God the beloved's salvation is what it means to be a neighbor to the next person met.

The Liberation of Power

Religious imperatives are maddeningly vague. They only become concrete on the road from Jerusalem to Jericho. Each new situation provides the raw material for creative acts of loving.

But love does not just happen. It takes ingenuity and, properly understood, skull-duggery. Creative loving means knowing the price of salvation and finding a way to pay it. Jesus suggested that it is foolish to announce plans for a twelve-story building when you only have materials for five stories; and if you are planning to wage a war against a king with ten thousand men while you only have five thousand men, you had better sue for peace. Loving the neighbor is costly. The exact cost will shift from situation to situation; but it will most likely entail an expenditure of power.

An overlooked phrase of the double commandment is that we are to love God with all our might. One interpretation is that means whatever constitutes our power. It could include money, property, position, charisma, time, knowledge—whatever gives us leverage in life.

In other words, we are to put all we are in the service of divine love. Power is a relative reality.[27] It has many different understandings and an infinitely diverse amount of embodiments, from presidents to legislators to paper carriers. But everyone has power. We all generate influence in the diverse situations of our lives. Even a first-grader has a kindergarten kid to push around. Loving God with all our might and our neighbor as ourselves means a specific use of power, power as service to the next person met.

A limited, but interesting, way to explore power as service is to trace the disagreements Jesus had with his disciples, especially with Peter. In almost all the conflicts Jesus had with his disciples (and he had many), the issue of power and authority was present: "When [Jesus] was in the house, he asked them, 'What were you arguing about on the way?' But they were silent, for on the way they had argued with one another who was the greatest" (Mark 9:33–34). Peter is the special foil for Jesus' views on a loving use of power. In Matthew 16:13–20, Peter recognizes the source of Jesus' power is his appropriation of true Sonship. Jesus is the Son of the Living God. He is rewarded for this insight, which is credited not to himself but to God's gift, with the keys to the kingdom. Peter and, by implication, the others now have the power which accrues to the accepting of divine love. The type of power that divine love generates will prove to be more a demand than a privilege. Further episodes reveal the radical nature of this power.

In the very next incident in the Gospel of Matthew (16:21–23), the conflict between Jesus and Peter about the use of power begins. Jesus predicts that he will go up to Jerusalem where he will be put to death and rise on the third day. Peter will have none of it: "God forbid it, Lord! This must never happen to you." For this sincere display of concern, Peter is called Satan and told to get back into the following of Jesus, to allow Jesus to show the way.

Peter knows that Jesus is the Son of Power; and he knows how power works. Power is for the purpose of exempting yourself from the fate which the powerless have to undergo. The sons of kings never die in the wars their fathers start. The daughters of legislators are never ground up in the tax laws their mothers enact. Those in power use it to secure themselves against the factors which would diminish them.

In this context, it is certainly folly for the Son of Ultimate Power to submit to the conditions of powerlessness. But Jesus is redefining the understanding and use of power. Power embraces the conditions of life in a new way; it does not exempt itself. The power that flows from divine love is not armor, but increased vulnerability, an openness to life which will overcome its destructiveness by undergoing it.

A second episode that contains a conflict about power is Matthew 18:21–22. Peter, knowing that Jesus is forgiveness prone, offers a generous estimate of how many times our brothers and sisters should be forgiven. "As many as seven times?" In this interchange, his rebuke is milder but just as undercutting. "Not seven times, but, I tell you, seventy-seven times."

There is more here than just the contrast between a definite number and an infinite capacity. Peter has the keys and what good are keys unless you can lock some people in and others out. Power only knows itself as power when it excludes. Until it excommunicates, it is never sure that it is communicating. Peter is subtly asking when he can exercise his power and exclude. Jesus' rejoinder is questioning his assumption. Power is not for the purposes of exclusion. It is for the mission of inclusion. The power that flows from loving God with all your might brings people together; it does not tear them apart.

A third episode, and the most famous conflict between Jesus and Peter, is recorded in the thirteenth chapter of the Gospel of John. Jesus is washing the feet of the disciples. Peter refuses this service. Jesus says that if Peter does not allow himself to be washed he will have nothing in common with him. The impetuous Peter then requests an entire bath.

The disconcerting factor in the story is initially that the master has become the servant. The lesson is not lost on Peter. If Jesus who is the master acts like this, what does it say about Peter's use of his authority and power. Peter's reluctance would seem to stem from the fact that this feet-washing is a prophecy for his own life.

But the issue of power in the story goes beyond the mere fact of reversal. It is what Jesus has chosen to serve that is the core of Peter's balking. The master serves concrete human needs. Dirty feet are the objects of his ministrations. But the rhetoric of service that abounds in the Christian church is often more noble than this. Service is given to the kingdom, the idealized social order, the vision of the future. And when this is what is served, a crushed body is tolerated, a mangled spirit is surely an acceptable price. Divine love not only demands that power serve but demands that it serve concrete human need.

Two short episodes in Luke (9:49–50; 9:51–56) further specify the use of power. John tells Jesus that the disciples met a man who was casting out devils in his name and they told him to stop. The reason that they urged the man to stop was that "he was not one of us."

John expects to be commended by Jesus. Instead he is rebuked. "You must not stop him. Anyone who is not against you is for you." Power often wants to stop goodness if it cannot get anything out of it. It wants to control the good. If it cannot be attributed to our group, then it must be stopped. The bolstering of the group takes precedence over salvific action. The fact that now there lives a person free of demons is insignificant. The matter of importance is that we have not worked this wonder. This tendency to usurp the good and to deny it where it cannot be usurped is a distortion of the overflowing power of divine love.

The disciples went on ahead to make preparations in a Samaritan village. The Samaritans would not receive them. James and John suggested to Jesus that he call down fire from heaven and burn them up. Jesus suggested that they find another village. The tendency of power is to use it for revenge. If we have been rejected, reject back—only harder. Lack of hospitality is met by cremation. The way of power is retribution. The disciples know this, but Jesus knows something different. Power is invitation to new life; and when it is rejected, it seeks other opportunities. The preoccupation of power is not violence but creative invitation.

The consequence of experiencing God as Love and ourselves as daughters and sons of Love is the freedom to use our power to serve the neighbor. Since we have ultimately grounded ourselves in God and not in our own efforts, our powers are redirected. They are creatively released for "kingdom" activity.

This means that we do not use power to exempt ourselves from the conditions of life, but to embrace those conditions in an effort to transform them; that we do not use power to exclude, but to include; that we do not dedicate our talents to the service of abstract ideals, but to real human needs; that we use our authority to allow the good to flourish and not to co-opt it; that we use whatever position we have to create opportunities and not to avenge ourselves on others. Once human power has been regrounded in divine love, it has a radically different agenda. Loving God with all our might means placing our power at the service of our neighbor, as the following story demonstrates.

When we think of loving the neighbor as ourselves, we immediately feel the challenge is to love the stranger. It is taken for granted that we will love family and friends. But the truth is that the next person we meet is easier to love than the ones we meet every day. In his fascinating book, *The Silence of Jesus,* James Breech suggests that it is those who eat with us who become the test of love.

> Many people would be willing to sacrifice their lives, if necessary, out of "love" for another. But such acts of immediate heroism which occur as it were on a stage with everyone watching, and which terminate the ordeal of living in the presence of the concrete other, are not to be confused with love of neighbor, which means hard work and tenacity, and which involves learning to affirm the actual other who sits across from one at the table, whether his or her table manners are graceful or ungraceful, his or her conversation engaging or boring, his or her habits mannerly or ill-mannered. The prayer that Jesus taught his table companions to say before sitting down to eat and drink together shows that Jesus understood the fundamental dynamics of such occasions, that it was during that time, as perhaps at no other, that they were most in need of that power which would sustain them in their readiness to be present in fellowship.[28]

If this is true, it is fitting to close our exploration of the experience of Spirit, the interwoven reality of divine and human love, with a story about the love of neighbor. Not the neighbor in the ditch but the neighbor at the table.

Why Bother?

"Why bother?" is what Margaret Mary Mulligan told her husband, Michael Joseph Mulligan, in June 1948 when, upon his retirement from Sears after thirty years, he proposed they take their granddaughter, who had just graduated from grammar school, and go back to Ireland to see his oldest brother. Margaret, as was her custom, repeated her opinion. "Why bother?"

But when he told his granddaughter, she was delighted and asked, "Gramp, are you and Gram going to go back to live in Ireland."

"Why should I?" he answered without taking the pipe out of his mouth. "I starved there."

And indeed he had. He was the second son of four sons and three daughters. His older brother was obviously in line for the farm. That was the way it was. There was not much for him and the others to do but move along. And the sooner the better. For what food there was would go farther with one less. So, as he likes to tell it, he threw his shoes over his shoulder to save the wear and tear, walked barefoot over the mountain, and got on the boat for America. That was May 1908.

First, there was a series of jobs in New York—stock boy, wagon driver, street repairman, a humiliating stint as a servant—"Hey, Paddy, get the dog." Then he took a chance. He moved to Chicago and with some luck and a good word from a cousin's cousin he landed a steady job at Sears. He met Margaret and settled down. Three children came along, but so did the Great Depression. The little prosperity they had was wiped out.

But with careful planning—scrimping here and saving there—he got back on his feet. Just as he was standing up, he looked around to find out he was old. When it was his wife Margaret's turn to speak at the retirement party, she said, "Ah, Mike, where did it all go? Where did it all go?"

Through the years Michael Thomas Mulligan kept in touch

with his older brother. Every year at Christmas he wrote a letter telling the news he could remember. He was not much of a letter writer, and so his yearly epistles often began, "Not much new here." But he always sent a check. After the first of the year a return letter would arrive. More often than not it began, "Not much new here either." The check was never mentioned.

But in June 1948, the day after Margaret had said, Why bother?" he wrote a letter out of season. "Margaret, I, and our granddaughter are coming to Ireland for a visit. Would you be home on July 11 in the evening?" A return letter arrived on the last day of June, one day before the train to New York and three days before the sailing to Ireland. It read: "I would. We will be expecting you for dinner."

On July 11, Michael Thomas Mulligan, the second son of four sons and three daughters, rented the newest model Packard he could find, put on this three piece, broad-lapelled, broad-striped suit, placed his large gold watch in the pocket of his vest and ran the gold chain prominently to the vest pocket, looked approvingly at his wife, Margaret, in her best hat and dress, and told his granddaughter, "No pedal pushers. I want you to wear a dress." He was on his way to see his older brother.

The stone and thatch cottage was much like he remembered it. Only it seemed farther from the main road and by the time they got there the car was covered with mud. It might as well have been a '32 Ford. Gerald John Mulligan and his wife stood at the door. "Jerry," said the younger brother with his hand extended. "Mike," said the older brother taking it. Their eyes never met. Inside the table was already set.

The dinner was plain and good. The talk was general—about the brothers and sisters, America, children, Ireland, the war. The granddaughter escaped to the room where she was to sleep as soon as she could. She propped herself up with a pillow and began reading a Nancy Drew mystery. Not much later the wives, sensing they should, said good night. The two brothers sat alone. After some time the older brother broke the silence.

"Are you now a rich Yank?"

"I am not," said the younger brother. "Are you now a prosperous land owner?"

"I am not," said the older brother.

The older brother stood up, moved to the cabinet, got a large loaf of fresh bread and a knife, and sat down. The younger brother stood up and went to the back bedroom. Margaret lay on one bed and his granddaughter, peering into a book, lay on the other. "Is it all right with him?" Margaret asked. "Get some rest," her husband said. He opened the suitcase and rummaged his arm under the neatly folded clothes. His hand brought out a quart bottle of Kentucky bourbon. "Is it all right with him?" she said again. "Get some rest," he said. But he smiled; and for the first time since they arrived in Ireland, she thought she might.

In the kitchen sat the two brothers and between them the bread the older brother had wrested from the stubborn land and the bottle the younger brother had brought back from the far country.

The first up in the morning was the granddaughter. She tiptoed out of the room without waking her grandmother. The kitchen table was filled with crumbs. In the middle of the crumbs was a knife and an empty bottle. The door to the cottage was open. She took it as an invitation and went outside.

The new day had just begun. The sun was climbing into the clear sky. It shimmered off the ocean in the distance and lit the land all the way up to the cottage. In the middle of the field stood the two brothers, pipes in their mouths, inspecting the earth the way a mother checks a newborn baby. "They must have been up all night," the granddaughter thought to herself.

Then the brothers turned, saw her, and waved. And side by side, stride by stride, step by step, they came toward her; and although she herself had never yet stayed up all night to beat back the darkness with her love, she knew that when her time came she would be able to do it. And when they came within earshot, she shouted out to them, "O Wow! You made it all the way to morning!"

For Further Response

1. Search through the "files" of your own personal experience and retrieve a "family" story similar to the one that ends this book.
2. Recount and record stories of temptations overcome.
3. Love one's neighbor may be easier said than done. How is love of God truly embedded in love of neighbor. How should this principle be applied to problem's of today's world?

Notes

Chapter One

1. Romano Guardini, "The Church: Encounter With Christ," in *The Church* (New York: P. J. Kenedy & Sons, 1963), p. 28.
2. Quoted in Yves Congar, *The Meaning of Tradition* (New York: Hawthorn Books, 1964), p. 16.
3. Robert Browning, "A Death in the Desert" in *The Poems and Plays of Robert Browning* (New York: The Modern Library, 1934), p. 297.
4. Walter Kasper, *Jesus the Christ* (New York: Paulist Press, 1976), p. 28.
5. John Coventry, *Christian Truth* (New York: Paulist Press, 1975). p. 65.
6. Cf. David Tracy, *The Analogical Imagination* (New York: Crossroad, 1981), pp. 236–241.
7. Willie Marxsen, *The Beginnings of Christology: A Study in Its Problems* (Philadelphia: Fortress Press, 1969), p. 20–21.
8. Cf. Edward Schillebeeckx, *Interim Report on the Books Jesus & Christ* (New York: Crossroad, 1981), p. 12.
9. Willie Marxsen, *The New Testament As the Church's Book* (Philadelphia: Fortress Press, 1972), p. 92.
10. Edward Schillebeeckx, *God and Man* (New York: Sheed and Ward, 1969), p. 164.
11. John Bowker, *The Religious Imagination and the Sense of God* (Oxford: Clarendon Press, 1978), p. 126.
12. Boniface Willems, *The Reality of Redemption* (New York: Herder and Herder, 1970), p. 61.

13. David Stanley, "Contemplation of the Gospels, Ignatius Loyola, and the Contemporary Christian," in *Theological Studies*, Vol. 29, No. 3, p. 425.

14. Cf. Ernst Kasemann, *The Testament of Jesus: A Study of the Gospel of John in the Light of Chapter Seventeen* (London: SCM Press, 1968).

15. Ray Brown, *The Gospel According to John* (New York: Doubleday & Company, Inc., 1966), p. 1139.

16. James D. G. Dunn, *Jesus and the Spirit* (Philadelphia: The Westminster Press, 1975), p. 351.

17. G. W. H. Lampe, *God As Spirit* (Oxford, 1977), p. 144.

18. Dunn, *Jesus and the Spirit*, p. 351.

19. Often experience and consciousness are distinguished. We may be experiencing something, but not be aware of it. The most obvious example is blood. We are constantly experiencing the nourishing effects of our blood; but we seldom explicitly focus on it and bring it to the level of awareness. We will not be consistently employing this distinction. When we use the word *experience*, it will refer to conscious experience.

20. D. E. H. Whiteley, *The Theology of St. Paul* (Oxford: Basil Blackwell, 1964), p. 197.

21. There is much discussion about the connection of metaphor and reality. Sometimes they are contrasted as this statement from the "Faith and Order Report" at Lund: "The Pauline image of the Church as the body of Christ is no mere metaphor, but expresses a living reality." This report is cited by G. C. Berkouwer who comments that this contrast between metaphor and reality is an "unenlightening dilemma...because there cannot be a contradiction between figurative language and reality: figurative language undoubtedly intends to refer to reality. A metaphor is not a vague, unreal expression, but intends, in the service of revelation, to open one's eyes to a deep, fascinating reality. And so, the question is not 'real or not real?' but is directed to the nature of the reality that is pointed out." *Studies in Dogmatics: The Church* (Grand Rapids, MI: William B. Eerdmans, 1976), p. 81.

22. Edward Schillebeeckx, *Christ: The Experience of Jesus As Lord* (New York: Crossroad, 1980), p. 19.

23. Our investigation does not take into account the reports of saints
   and mystics that they were visited by the Risen Lord. These reports are fascinating and open to many diverse interpretations.
   But they seem to be the privilege of the few. We are exploring the
   more accessible mode of the presence of Christ—through the
   people animated by his Spirit. We are also not considering, in
   any detail, the relationship between the Risen Lord and the Spirit.
   For our purpose it is enough to say that the Risen Lord sends the
   Spirit and that the presence of the Spirit mediated the presence of
   the Risen Lord. For a fuller treatment consult Peter C. Hodgson,
   New Birth of Freedom (Philadelphia: Fortress Press, 1976), pp.
   324–332.
24. Quoted in Gerald O'Collins, *Fundamental Theology* (New York:
   Paulist Press, 1981), p. 209.
25. Cf. James D. G. Dunn, *Unity and Diversity in the New Testament* (Philadelphia: The Westminster Press, 1977), pp. 192–193.
26. Ibid., p. 194.
27. Congar, *The Meaning of Tradition*, p. 148.
28. Northrop Frye, *The Great Code* (New York: Harcourt Brace
   Jovanovich, 1981), p. 128.
29. Quoted in Robert Funk, *Language, Hermeneutic, and Word of
   God* (New York: Harper & Row, 1966), introductory quote.
30. Spirit and Memory are more than critical correctives. They are
   also mutual partners in bringing about the experience of Spirit.
   We will investigate this partnership in chapter three.

Chapter Two

1. David Tracy, *The Analogical Imagination* (New York: Crossroad,
   1981), p. 249.
2. Teilhard de Chardin, *Hymn to the Universe* (New York: Harper
   & Row, 1961), p. 48.
3. Cf. Larry D. Shinn, *Two Sacred Worlds* (Nashville: Abingdon,
   1977), chapter three.
4. John Macquarrie, *Principles of Christian Theology* (New York:
   Charles Scribner's Sons, 1966), pp. 92–93.
5. Paul Tillich, *Systematic Theology*, Vol. 1 (Chicago: University of
   Chicago Press, 1951), pp. 126–28.

6. Cf. Charles Davis, *Body As Spirit* (New York: Seabury Press, 1976), chapter one.
7. For a clear theory of how this happens which is indebted to the philosophy of Suzanne K. Langer, cf. Ronald J. Alien, "Feeling and Form in Biblical Interpretation," *Encounter*, Vol. 43, No. 1, Winter, 1982.
8. For an example of this type of acculturation of belief, confer Charles Meyer, *Religious Belief in a Scientific Age* (Chicago: Thomas More Press, 1983).
9. Cf. John Shea, *Stories of God* (Chicago: Thomas More Press, 1978), chapter one.
10. Cf. Friedrich Nietzche, *Beyond Good and Evil: A Philosophy for the Future*, translated by Walter Kaufman (New York: Random House, 1966).
11. For a good explanation of pervasive attitudes confer Donald Evans, *Struggle and Fulfillment* (Cleveland: Collins, 1976).
12. Cf. Ray Hart, *Unfinished Man and the Imagination* (New York: Herder and Herder, 1966), pp. 143–51.

Chapter Three

1. Johann Baptist Metz, *Faith in History and Society* (New York: Seabury Press, 1980), p. 210.
2. In the first chapter we suggested that Spirit and Memory must be held in tension as the Christian people journey through and time. They act as critical correctives to the dangerous space tendencies in each other. This chapter explores their partnership, the way they work together to facilitate the experience of Spirit.
3. A helpful contrast of these two sets of triggers can be found in James Joyce's *A Portrait of the Artist As A Young Man* (New York: B. W. Huebsch, 1916). The long and terrifying retreat cannot move Stephen's soul. The traditional facilitators of religious experience are bankrupt. But at the stream at Clontarf he sees the young girl and exclaims, "Heavenly God!...He turned away from her suddenly and set off the strand. His cheeks were aflame; his body was aglow; his limbs were trembling. On and on and on he strode, far out over the sands, singing wildly to the sea, crying to greet the advent of life that had cried to him" (pp. 199–200).

4. R. Stark, "A Taxonomy of Religious Experience," *Journal for the Scientific Study of Religion*, 1965, 5, pp. 98–116.
5. Cf. John Shea, *Stories of Faith* (Chicago: Thomas More Press, 1980), chapters one and two.
6. Quoted in Edward Robinson, *The Original Vision* (Manchester College, Oxford: The Religious Experience Research Unit, 1977), p. 148.
7. Walter Gulick, "Archetypal Experiences," *Soundings*, Fall 1981, p. 262.
8. Yves Congar, *The Meaning of Tradition* (New York: Hawthorn Books, 1964), p. 75.
9. Cf. Ian Barbour, *Myths, Models, and Paradigms* (New York: Harper & Row, 1974), Chapter Four.
10. Ernest Hemingway, *The Old Man and the Sea* (New York: Scribner's, 1952), p. 107.
11. Cf. George W. Stroup, *The Promise of Narrative Theology* (Atlanta: John Knox Press, 1981), Part II, Christian Identity.
12. Cf. C. Daniel Batson, J. Christiaan Beker, and W. Malcolm Clark, *Commitment Without Ideology* (Philadelphia: United Church Press, 1973), chapter three.
13. This story was related at a faith and storytelling seminar.
14. Quoted in Robinson, pp. 69–70.
15. Cf. John Shea, "Religious-Imaginative Encounters with Scriptural Stories," in *Art/Literature/Religion: Life on the Borders* (Chico, CA: Scholars Press, 1983), pp. 173–80.
16. Norman Perrin, *Jesus and the Language of the Kingdom* (Philadelphia: Fortress Press, 1976), Part II: The Interpretation of Kingdom of God in the Message of Jesus.
17. Cf. G. B. Caird, *The Language and Imagery of the Bible* (Philadelphia: The Westminster Press, 1980), chapter ten.
18. Ibid., p. 145

Chapter Four

1. Nikos Kazantzakis, *The Greek Passion* (New York: Simon and Schuster, 1953), p. 429.
2. Cf. Norman Perrin, *Rediscovering the Teachings of Jesus* (New York: Harper & Row, 1967), chapter five.
3. Cf. Birger Gerhardsson, *The Testing of God's Son* (Lund: Coniectanea Biblica, 1966).
4. Cf. James Breech, *The Silence of Jesus* (Philadelphia: Fortress Press, 1983), pp. 46–49.
5. Cf. Robert Tannehill, *The Sword of His Mouth* (Philadelphia: Fortress Press, 1975), pp. 11–36.
6. Sebastian Moore, *The Crucified Jesus Is No Stranger* (New York: Seabury Press. 1977); *The Fire and the Rose Are One* (New York: Seabury Press, 1980); *The Inner Loneliness* (New York: Crossroad, 1982). All three of these books are profound meditations on human sinfulness and divine redemption.
7. Moore, *The Fire and the Rose*, p. 11.
8. Ibid., p. 13.
9. Ibid., p. 37.
10. Cf. John Shea, *Stories of Faith* (Allen, TX: Thomas More Publishing, 1980), chapter two.
11. James Mackey, *Jesus: The Man and the Myth* (New York: Paulist Press, 1979), p. 170.
12. Cf. Ben Meyer, *The Aims of Jesus* (SCM Press, LTD) and John Riches, *Jesus and the Transformation of Judaism* (London: Darton, Longman & Todd, 1980).
13. This is not an attempt at a sociological analysis or a suggestion that the complexity of sin can be reduced to these two options. It merely points to two "wrong centerings" as types of responses the panicked inner self is prone to.
14. Meyer, *The Aims of Jesus*, p. 161.
15. Mackey, *Jesus: The Man and the Myth*, pp. 143–44.
16. Paul Ricoeur, "Biblical Hermeneutics," *Semeia* (1975).
17. Dorothy Sollee has some interesting reflections on testing in *Suffering* (Philadelphia: Fortress Press, 1973), chapter four.
18. Gerhardsson, *The Testing of God's Son*, p. 31.

Chapter Five

1. Idries Shah, *The Way of the Sufi* (New York: E. P. Dutton, 1968), p. 63.
2. William James, "The Divided Self and Conversion," in *Conversion*, ed., Walter E. Conn (New York: Alba House, 1978), p. 128.
3. Ibid.
4. Donald Evans, *Struggle and Fulfillment* (New York: Collins, 1979), p. 53.
5. Cf. Kenneth E. Bailey, *Through Peasant Eyes* (Grand Rapids, MI: William B. Eerdmans, 1980).
6. John Cobb, *The Structure of Christian Existence* (Philadelphia: The Westminster Press, 1968), p. 135.
7. Cf. Victor Paul Furnish, *The Love Command in the New Testament* (New York: Abingdon Press, 1972), chapter four.
8. Don E. Saliers, *The Soul in Paraphrase* (New York: A Crossroad Book, 1980), p. 71.
9. Cf. Jon Sobrino, *Christology at the Crossroads* (Maryknoll, New York: Orbis Books, 1978).
10. Norman Perrin, *Rediscovering the Teachings of Jesus* (New York: Harper & Row, 1967), p. 94.
11. Nikos Kazantzakis, *Report to Greco* (New York: Simon and Schuster, 1976).
12. Anne Sexton, *The Awful Rowing Toward God* (Boston: Houghton Mifflin Company, 1975), pp. 85–86.
13. Cf. Birger Gerhardsson, *The Testing of God's Son* (CWK Gleerup Lund Sweden, 1966); John A. T. Robinson, *Twelve New Testament Studies* (Naperville, IL: Alec R. Allenson, Inc., 1962), pp. 53–60.
14. Edward Schillebeeckx, *Christ: The Sacrament of the Encounter With God* (New York: Sheed & Ward, 1963), p. 18.
15. Donald Evans, *Struggle and Fulfillment* (New York: Collins, 1979).
16. Ibid., p. 23.
17. James Mackey, *Jesus: The Man and the Myth* (New York: Paulist Press, 1979), pp. 192–93.

18. Henri J. M. Nouwen, ¡*Gracias! A Latin American Journal* (San Francisco: HarperCollins Publishers, 1983), p. 120.

19. Quoted in Mary Gordon, *Final Payments* (New York: Ballantine Books, 1978), p. 232.

20. Ibid., p. 260.

21. Gunther Bornkamm, *Jesus of Nazareth* (New York: Harper & Row, 1960), p. 111.

22. Cf. C. Daniel Batson and W. Larry Ventis, *The Religious Experience* (New York: Oxford University Press, 1982), chapter three.

23. Quoted in Bornkamm, *op. cit.*, p. 113.

24. Max Scheler, *The Nature of Sympathy* (Hamden, CT.: Shoe String Press, 1973), p. 121.

25. Quoted in Furnish, *The Love Command in the New Testament*, p. 210.

26. Edward V. Vacek, "Scheler's Phenomenology of Love" in *The Journal of Religion*, Vol. 62 (April, 1982), p. 167.

27. Confer the diverse and fascinating attempts to reflect on power theologically in "The Proceedings of the Thirty-Seventh Annual Convention of the Catholic Theological Society of America," Luke Salm, ed.

28. Breech, *The Silence of Jesus*, p. 61.

Acknowledgments and Permissions

James P. Mackey, multiple citations from *Jesus: The Man and the Myth* by James P. Mackey. Copyright © 1979 by James P. Mackey. Used by permission of the Paulist Press.

Henri J. M. Nouwen, from ¡*Gracias! A Latin American Journal* by Henri J. M. Nouwen. Copyright © 1983 by Henri J. M. Nouwen. Reprinted by permission of HarperCollins Publishers, Inc., San Francisco.

Anne Sexton, "The Rowing Endeth," from *The Awful Rowing Toward God* by Anne Sexton. Copyright 1975 by Loring Conant, Jr., Executor of the Estate of Anne Sexton; *The Death Notebooks* by Anne Sexton. Copyright © 1974 by Anne Sexton. Reprinted by permission of Houghton Mifflin Company. All rights reserved.

Edward Robinson, from *The Original Vision*, used by permission of and copyright 1977 by The Religious Experience Research Unit, Manchester College, Oxford, England.

Scripture citations are taken from the *New Revised Standard Version of the Bible*, copyright 1989 by the Division of Christian Education of the National Council of the Churches of Christ in the USA. All rights reserved. Used with permission.

About the Author

JOHN SHEA is a theologian and storyteller who lectures nationally and internationally on storytelling in world religions, faith-based health care, contemporary spirituality, and the spirit at work movement. Currently, he is the Director of Programs and Developmental Processes for the Ministry Leadership Center, headquartered in Sacramento, California. Formerly, he was a professor of systematic theology and the Director of the Doctor of Ministry Program at the University of St. Mary of the Lake, a research professor at the Institute of Pastoral Studies at Loyola University of Chicago, and the Advocate Healthcare Senior Scholar in Residence at the Park Ridge Center for the Study of Health, Faith and Ethics. He has also taught at the University of Notre Dame and Boston College. He has published fifteen books of theology and spirituality and two books of poetry. His latest book, the first of a four volume series, is *The Spiritual Wisdom of the Gospels for Christian Preachers and Teachers*: Vol. 1, *On Earth As It Is in Heaven* (Liturgical Press, 2004).